THE

EDUCATION

OF A

CHILD.

FROM

THE WISDOM OF FENELON.

EDITED AND REWRIT
BY MARK

LAMPLIGHTER PUBLISHING
PO BOX 777, WAVERLY, PA 18471

THE EDUCATION OF A CHILD.

Copyright © 2000, Mark Hamby
Cover Design Copyright © 2000
First Printing, October, 2000

Published by Lamplighter Publishing; a division of Cornerstone Family Ministries, Inc. For more information, contact: P.O. Box 777, Waverly, PA 18471 or call 1-888-A-GOSPEL.

Author: Francois de Salignac de La Mothe Fenelon, 17th century
Translator: Benedict Rayment, 1805
Editor: Mark Hamby

Printed in the United States of America

ISBN 1-58474-055-8

CONTENTS.

Preface.

I thank the Lord that I have been so wonderfully blessed by allowing me to glean such grand eternal truths, from such a wise and godly master teacher. Francois Fenelon was a French citizen, the archbishop of Cambray, during the seventeenth century. He was a descendent of a noble military family of Perigord, and was often surrounded by the simplicity of country life, well-protected from the fashionable extremes and the haughty air of the courts. His father, Pons de Salignac, Comte de Fenelon, retired from the army, and married Isabelle d'Esparbes, by whom he had several children. As a widower somewhat advanced in years, he entered into a second alliance with Louise de Saint-Abre, sister of Marquis de Saint-Abre, the daughter of a noble family in the same province. This union was the cause of much annoyance to his children, who murmured against the conduct of their father. They feared that the probable increase of family members would so diminish the inheritance of each, as to cause their decline from the high rank they had counted as theirs. Antoine de Fenelon, the uncle of these young benefactors, having been informed of their complaints, wrote to his nephews, rebuking their opposition in a letter which has been preserved amid the family archives.

"Learn," said he, "to bow with deference and respect to the wishes of your father: Providence has ever its secret intentions, unfathomable to the eyes of men. Often the fortune and exaltation of a house proceed from causes opposed to the desires of our short-sighted wisdom." It might have been said that this uncle foresaw in the child yet unborn, the lasting glory of their name.

The first offspring of this marriage was Francois Fenelon. The son of an older father and a youthful mother, he was endowed with the mature wisdom of the one and the graces of the other. Cherished in the paternal mansion like a late and delicate fruit, till the age of twelve years, he was brought up beneath the eyes of his parents. As he grew to maturity, the clear sense of his father and the sweet tenderness of his mother reappeared in his mind, his conduct, and his writings.

Under a domestic preceptor, the first food offered to his imagination was the study of sacred literature, with the Greek and Latin classics. His heart and reason, thus modeled upon all that was good and beautiful in antiquity, naturally took a noble form and coloring. It may be said that though this child was in France during the seventeenth century, his genius was conceived at Athens in the age of Pericles. His education was finished at the University of Cahors. The fame of his brilliant qualities, resounding from the precincts of his school, reached the ears of Antoine de Fenelon, the same uncle who had proved so true an augur before the infant's birth. This relative, having now attained a high rank in the army, invited his nephew to join him in Paris. The youth was destined to the priesthood, being looked upon as a burden on the family, which they were desirous of transferring to the church. His philosophical and theological studies were pursued with increased success in the eminent schools of Paris. His natural, versatile, and precocious genius developed itself more brilliantly there than at Cahors, while his talents and graceful accomplishments gained the attachment of many eminent friends. The lustre of glory and admiration, by which the young Fenelon was surrounded, excited the apprehensions of his venerable uncle, who hastened to withdraw his nephew from the seductions of friendship and society, by sending him to the seminary of St. Sulpice.

While Fenelon pursued his sacred studies, his uncle, desirous of teaching his own son the rudiments of war, conducted him to the siege of Candia, against the Turks. The young man fell in the first assault, struck by a ball, and expired in his father's arms. The old warrior returned to Paris, bringing the body of his son. The loss of his only son attached Antoine de Fenelon still more strongly to his nephew. Good and pious himself, he desired for the young neophite no ecclesiastical honors, but only reward of piety and virtue.

The ardent imagination of young Fenelon carried him to the point of enthusiasm in his profession. He formed the resolution of leaving the cloister to enroll himself among the missionaries who were endeavoring to convert Canada to Christianity, and of consecrating his life like the first preachers of the Gospel, to the rescue of heathen souls in the forests of the New World. He was irresistibly attracted by the resemblance which the devotion and self-denial of the these modern Thebaids bore to the apostles of old. His ardent imagination from early youth, and throughout his entire existence, mingled itself with all his dreams, and even with his virtues. Thus, one destined to improve courts and to instruct monarchs, desired only to civilize savages in the solitude of a desert. Commanded by another uncle, the bishop of Sarlat, who solemnly forbade his embarkment upon this perilous enterprise, young Fenelon submitted and thus became a priest.

Though committed to his vows, Fenelon's earnest desire of becoming an errant apostle for the conversion of the heathen, remained fervent.

During the reign of terror of King Louis XIV against the protestants, Fenelon was nominated as Superior, to soothe the tensions among the dissenters and recanters. Religious warfare had scarcely been quelled in France, when the revocation of the Edict of Nantes struck a fatal blow at liberty of conscience, by violating the treaty between opposing creeds, solemnly accorded by Henry the Fourth. Three hundred thousand families were expelled, deprived of their children, and their property confiscated. Millions of others, in the Protestant provinces, were placed under constraint. Some were persuaded, others compelled by force, to renounce the religion of their fathers and adopt that of the State. In the part of the kingdom where Protestantism had taken its deepest root, great persecution was launched by both church and state; and armed with tongue and sword, they were brought back by zeal, seduction, or terror. This prosecution was executed primarily through the tyranny of Louis the fourteenth, having now become old and fanatical. He thought to gain heaven himself by offering to the church this vast spoil of souls, crushed and terrified under his authority.

No man was so capable of reassuring these terror-stricken people, of making the yoke imposed upon them appear light and easy, and of restoring amnesty of conscience in the provinces where persecution and preaching had so discreditably contended. At the first presentation of Fenelon to Louis the Fourteenth, the sole favor he demanded of the king was to disarm religion of all coercive power; to release Protestants from the terrors which petrified their souls, and to allow them once more to breathe; to banish troops from the provinces he was about to visit; and to let persuasion, charity, and mercy alone operate upon the minds he desired rather to enlighten than to subdue. Charmed by Fenelon's grace, modesty, and eloquence, Louis the Fourteenth, who cared little for the means that were adopted, allowed Fenelon to proceed.

During this period in history, where the overthrow of thrones still overshadowed the monarch's crown, Louis the Fourteenth, obsessed with uncontrolled jealousy, banished his son to Meudon, where he resided, almost in a state of indigence. The king trembled less before the shadow of death than before the knowledge that one day he must cease to reign. The Duke of Burgandy, the guidance of whose studies had been confided to Fenelon, was the grandson of the king, who, following the custom of grandfathers, preferred this child to his own son. His extreme youth removed all unpleasant feelings, as the great disparity of years placed a wide distance between the monarch's reign and that of this youthful successor.

Such was the Court of France when Fenelon entered upon his functions as preceptor to the Duke of Burgandy. The first thoughts of Fenelon upon attaining his new honours, were directed to friendship. He appointed two of his honorable friends and one nephew, the

Abbe Fleury, and the Abbe de Beaumont (his nephew), sub-preceptors to the young prince; and to the Abbe de Langeron he assigned the office of reader. Thus he concentrated all his affections in his employment, and multiplied around his pupil the same spirit under different names. The destiny of this child, confided to Fenelon, was the future fate of a nation. The disposition of this child, however, inspired more fear than hope. "He was terrible from birth," said one Simon. "In his earliest years he caused those about him to tremble; unfeeling, displaying the most violent passion, which extended towards inanimate objects, incapable of bearing the slightest contradiction, even from the hours or the elements, without giving way to a whirlwind of rage sufficient to break all the blood-vessels in his body—I speak of what I have often witnessed: opinionated to excess; absorbed in the pursuits of pleasure, fond of good living, following the chase with furious impetuosity, enjoying music with a sort of delirium, madly attached to play, but unable to bear loss, and when defeated, becoming positively dangerous; in fact, abandoned to all the evil passions, and transported by every corrupting pleasure; often savage, naturally cruel; bitter in raillery, ridiculing with a remorseless power, regarding all men (irrespective of merit), from his high position, but as atoms with whom he could have no affinity. The extent and vivacity of his powers were so varied that they prevented his fixing upon any distinct branch of knowledge, and almost rendered him incapable of study. From this abyss came forth a prince." This prince was the child confided to Fenelon to remodel.

More powerful than his philosophy of education were the two attributes he possessed most requisite in those who teach—the power of command and the gift of pleasing. To secure the affection of children, Fenelon believed that the authority of a father should be qualified with the tenderness of a mother. Dignity and fascination emanated from his whole being—nature had traced in his lineaments the beauty of his soul. His countenance expressed his genius even in moments of silence. The genius of Fenelon soared far above this circle; but we have already said that no man could so well adapt himself to those whom he could never raise to his own height. The greatest triumph of his genius consisted in forgetting itself.

The first process adopted by Fenelon toward his young pupil was the influence of his own character. He succeeded in persuading because he had succeeded in making himself loved, at first sterile and unproductive, but afterwards ductile and fruitful, into the Germanicus of France. It was in the midst of the studious leisure of this royal education, which forced upon Fenelon's mind the contemplation of the philosophy of societies, that he secretly composed, in a poetical form, his moral code of education—the classic, *Telemachus*. It is the wisdom of *Telemachus* which perpetuates the genius of Fenelon to all posterity. This book, which was in truth composed expressly for the young prince, was evidently written with the intention of fortifying his mind, when formed by manhood against the doctrines of tyranny and the snares of voluptuousness—pictures which the master presented to his pupil to arm him beforehand against the seductions of a throne, and the allurements of his own heart.

Inspired by the ancient Egyptians, Hebrews, and Greeks, Fenelon's philosophical approach for this educational endeavor was thoroughly based on the foundational principles of virtue. Virtue to Fenelon was understood in a classical sense, which included the eleven moral virtues of courage, temperance, liberality, magnificence, magnanimity, honour, gentleness, truthfulness, wittiness, friendliness and justice. *(cf. Aristotle, "Nichomachean Ethics", 2.7.)*

These precepts and experiences prepared Fenelon to write *The Education of a Daughter*. The title has been changed to *The Education of a Child*, because the tenor of thought and versatile application lends itself to the instruction of all children, for all ages, even though its focus is upon children of younger ages. A literal translation of an original first-edition manuscript was used in this edition and meticulously edited to retain the eloquence of this master. Editor's notes enhance difficult portions, and a second translation is used for clarity of thought where vocabulary necessitated distinction. Words and grammar have so evolved that to print this book in its original form could cause unnecessary strain to comprehend thoughts of long ago.

In the translation of this first-edition manuscript, written by Benedict Rayment, he harshly criticizes another editor for taking too much liberty in communicating Fenelon's thoughts and denounces its contents. To those who may find a copy of *The Education of a Daughter* by Fenelon in English form, its content, in all likelihood, is derived from this errant form; all one has to do is compare it to the depth of thought and the beauty and mastery of his words in this edition.

It is paradoxical that the such simple educational precepts and insights have been set aside for centuries and replaced with systems that continue to fail. It is almost as if the institutionalization of education, the removal of religion from public schools, and the disarming of moral truth, was understood to have been ordained by God. Have thinking people fallen asleep, anesthetized to the dire consequences of our present system, in both the secular and Christian arena of education? Such an attack may seem petty or lack sufficient grounds, but once Fenelon's philosophy of education is understood, present-day educators will begin to see how far we have strayed from the essential focus of education. According to Fenelon, academia without virtue trains a child to memorize without thinking, pursue without caring, and replaces passion and love for learning with boredom and fatigue. And shall we, who know God's indisputable instruction for a child's education, shrink from speaking truth in a century where incredulity is considered wisdom? Shall we blush at the mention of praise for that grace, that virtue, that cultivation of the soul, which so much lived in the heart of a man, who four centuries later still attracts those who are searching for direction based on the examination of tested waters? Of Fenelon's writings, it was stated in 1802 that they are the most perfect treatise upon education that exists in modern times.

Whatever your present philosophical prejudices, please place them aside for the moment and allow Fenelon to breathe into your soul at least a morsel of these simple but grand truths. Once realized, you will see how these truths expand the soul, warm the heart, elevate the genius, and give an energy to thought unknown to pagan antiquity. I respectfully submit to you a man's work, his passions, and his wisdom in this classic treatise, under its new title—*The Education of a Child.*

MARK HAMBY, EDITOR

The historical information in the preface was taken from two sources: *The Life of Fenelon* A. D. 1651—1715 by Lamartine, and the translator's preface from *The Education of a Daughter* by Benedict Rayment. Portions of the original manuscript not related to education have been omitted, with cautious discretion. Though I endorse the teachings of Fenelon on this subject, it does not suggest approval of his various other doctrines.

ON THE

EDUCATION

OF A

CHILD.

FROM THE WISDOM OF FENELON.

CHAP. I.

THE IMPORTANCE OF BESTOWING A GOOD EDUCATION ON DAUGHTERS.

It is the home that lays the foundation of a child's future. And though the strength of the foundation is determined by the virtues of both parents, it is a woman who holds the key to her children's heart in the early years of childhood. She has the privilege of weaving God's eternal truth into the daily lives of her children while they are still young and tender. A woman who is a mother, is she not greater than he that ruleth a city? Are not her children the foundations of all human life? Is it not women who attend to and support the whole domestic economy of our houses, and who decide upon what most intimately concerns mankind? A judicious woman, who is diligent and virtuous, is the soul of her family. She regulates and preserves its temporal and spiritual good. Men, who have even authority in public, cannot by their deliberation establish any effectual good, if they be not aided by women in the execution of it.

The world is not a mere phantom; it is an assemblage of families; and who can civilize and polish them with a care more exact than women, who by their natural authority, and diligence in their houses, possess the advantage of being more careful and attentive, more industrious, and persuasive? Can men hope to gain any happiness in life, if their closest connection, which is that of marriage, should be turned to bitterness? What will become of children, who will in the end form the human race, if their mothers spoil them in their early years? Behold, then, the duties of women, which are not less important to the public than those of men; since they have a house to regulate, a husband to render happy, and children to educate well: add also, that virtue is of no less importance to women than to men—without speaking of the good or evil they may cause to society—are they not half of the human race, especially those redeemed with the blood of Jesus Christ, and destined to eternal life?

Besides the good that women can affect who are well educated, and the evil they occasion in the world from an education which neglects to inspire them with virtue, it is evident that a bad education in women is productive of harmful and greater evils than that of men; for the vices of men can for the most part be traced back either to the evil influence or lack of influence of their mothers. The foundation of a child's life, is it not molded from the earliest days of his mother's breasts as he listens to the music of her heart? And is it not from this same heart that he will learn virtue or vice?

CHAP. II.

DEFECTS IN THE COMMON MODE OF EDUCATION.

The ignorance of a child is the cause of the weariness which he suffers, as he knows not how to occupy himself innocently; for after spending all the early part of life without any serious application, it is in vain to expect that he can have any taste or relish for any thing solid. Whatever is serious, appears to him dull;—whatever requires continued attention, fatigues him: the propensity to pleasure, which in youth is so strong, and the poor example of persons of the same age, who are plunged in amusements, all contribute to make him or her dread an orderly and industrious life. In their early years they want to be trusted but lack the experience and understanding necessary to undertake any share of the management of their parents' house; yet they know not even the importance of applying themselves to it responsibly, unless their mother have taken pains to exemplify these most noble and virtuous qualities and to point out these important duties to their inattentive eyes.

Mothers by nature are teachers; but a mother whose eye is ever upon her child, who is constantly scolding, thinking she is fulfilling her educative role in pardoning nothing, will oppress her child, specially those mothers (and fathers) who place the weight of the family concerns upon them; all of this only torments and discourages. Be on the alert also for companions who endeavour to insinuate themselves into their good graces, by indulging their whims and fancies; and thus, by means of their dangerous and designing conversations, they succeed in giving the child a disrelish of every thing that is good and serious: they make him look upon the practise of virtue as an occupation for gloomy minds, and an orderly life as the declared enemy of every enjoyment. By degrees this inapplication to any thing serious becomes an incurable habit. In what then will he or she employ themselves?—in nothing useful.

In this state of frivolity, if a child gives themselves up to idleness, which is the vacancy of the soul, exhausts himself into a state of weariness. These children often accustom themselves to sleep one-third more than is necessary for the preservation of health. This indulgence serves only to weaken, to undermine their constitution, and expose them to bodily infirmities, whereas a moderate degree of sleep, accompanied with regular exercise, exhilarates and renders the human frame vigorous and robust; which makes the true perfection of the body, without mentioning the vast advantage which the mind draws from it.

This softness and indolence of disposition, being blended with ignorance, gives rise to a pernicious sensibility, and a desire for public amusements; as it excites an indiscreet and insatiable curiosity, the enemy of the soul, and the mother of all evil.

Children well educated, who employ their minds on serious objects, have, for the most part, but an ordinary share of curiosity; what they know gives them a sovereign contempt for many things they wish not to know. They see the emptiness and the utility of the many things which the idle and the ignorant pursue with so much eagerness and passion.

Children ill instructed, and not accustomed to application, have wandering imaginations. For the want of solid nourishment to the mind, their curiosity turns towards objects which are vain and dangerous. Those who have wit, often become conceited, and read books which nourish their vanity; they become passionately fond of romances, comedies, and novels, which silently instil into their unguarded breasts the poison of profane love. These imaginary adventures render their minds visionary, in accustoming them to the strained sentiments of vain romantic heroes.

Children filled with thoughts of their romantic heroes, become astonished when they look around in real life, and cannot discover a single person throughout the world bearing resemblance with their ideal hero. They would wish to live like those princes and princesses who are always charming, always adored, always above every care. What a disgust for them to descend from a hero and heroine, to the low detail and drudgery of taking care of a family.

Children should be influenced by books that vividly portray life in all its trials and victories. Divine providence should echo throughout its pages. Characters who suffer wrongfully in a righteous manner, and display humble dispositions, will lay a secure foundation for the time when childhood may be stolen away; perhaps through the death of a loved one, sickness, or calamity. Children need informed instruction, and models of heroes and heroines of righteousness to fill their reserves for such a time. In literature as well as in history, God who doeth all things well, must be seen through the filter of His divine love and tender care for His children and as an avenger of all who harden their neck.

CHAP. III.

THE FIRST FOUNDATIONS OF A GOOD EDUCATION.

The early part of life, where the deepest impressions are made upon character, have a great influence on the remainder of life. Children must first be prepared for instruction before they have quite learned to speak. This, to some, may appear a little outre'. Consider, however, how, even in this tender age, children wish to go to those who please and flatter them, and shun those who lay any restraint upon them; how they can cry, or continue silent to obtain the objects of their desires, and what evident marks of cunning and jealousy is even at this age visible in their characters. "I have seen," says Augustine, "an infant so jealous that he could not speak; his countenance became so palid, his eyes sparkling with rage, as he looked upon another child that was suckling with him at the breast."

We may infer, that infants, even at that age, know more than is generally believed. Howsoever mischievous a child's natural disposition may be, it is yet easy to render it docile, patient, firm, joyful, and even tranquil; whereas, if it be neglected in its infancy, it becomes from thence self-willed, impetuous, and restless all its life. You may therefore give them by words, assisted with a certain tone of voice, which will instil into their tender minds a horror for anger, or any other disorderly passion they may have observed in others; and by a sweet tone and smiling countenance, impress them with admiration and love of whatever they have witnessed that is wise, good, or modest.

Beware of governesses and nurses who excite too strong emotions in children, with foolish imaginations, and an unbridled tongue. Our chief concern must be in giving them an agreeable and charming idea of virtue, and a frightful idea of vice; this early precaution would wonderfully facilitate the future practise of every virtue.

As soon as children arrive at the period of life when reason begins to assume the reigns, every word that is said to them should go to inspire a love of truth, and an abhorrence for all dishonesty. Thus we should never make use of any scheme or trick to appease them, or persuade them to do what we wish with, for by this we would teach them a sort of cunning and finesse, which they never forget. We ought to lead them, as much as possible, only by reason.

The pleasure we derive from pretty and engaging children, spoils them; they are encouraged by it to speak all that enters their mind, and of things of which they have no distinct knowledge. The effect of which is, that there remains with them for life, the habit of judging with precipitation, and of speaking of things of which they have no clear ideas: which stamps a bad character on the mind.

The entertainment which we derive from children, produces another bad effect upon them; they perceive that we notice them, that we observe all they do, that we hear them with pleasure: they are thus accustomed to believe that every body is occupied with them.

During this age wherein they are applauded, and in which they experience no contradiction, they are apt to acquire imaginary hopes, which prepare infinite disappointments for life. I have seen children who believed we spoke of them every time we conversed privately, because they had observed that we frequently spoke of them; they imagine that every thing in them is extraordinary and admirable. You must therefore be very attentive to children, without letting them observe that you are noticing them. Let them see that it is out of friendship, and the desire of their improvement, but by no means from an admiration of their talents, that you attend to them. Be content with forming their minds by degrees, according as occasions may present themselves; though you could advance a child very rapidly without forcing his capacity, you should still act very cautiously; for the danger of vanity and presumption ought to have greater weight in the scale than the glory of premature education, which is so much talked about. Balance compliments and encouragement with the knowledge that God is the source of all blessings. *For in Him we live and move and exist...* Acts xvii. 28.

Children know but little, we therefore must not encourage them to talk much; they are ignorant of most things, and have a thousand questions to ask. In this they are not to be discouraged. We must give them clear and precise answers, and add certain, easy comparisons, purposely to render our explanations more familiar. Never display the least displeasure at their childish enquiries; these are the overtures of nature, by which you may favourably instruct with pleasing tones. Let them see that you are pleased with their questions. You may be able thus to instruct them without their perceiving it, how all things are made which are necessary for the use of man, and what are the motives and springs of commerce. Thus, by degrees,and without any particular study, they will learn how every thing is made which they may hereafter want, and the exact price of each article, which is the first basis of true economy. This knowledge, which no one should despise, is necessary for the child to relate to the world around him. Spare not the time to stoop low enough to relate these principles of economy.

As soon as it shall appear that their reason has made some progress, we must make use of their experience to fortify them against presumption. You see, you will say to them, that you are more reasonable than you were a year ago; in another year you will know many more things than you do at present. If, a year ago, you had pretended to judge of those things which you now know but of which you were then ignorant, you would have judged erroneously. You would have been wrong in attempting to decide upon things of which you were ignorant. It is the same now with regard to subjects, of which you have yet to acquire a knowledge. You will one day see how very imperfect your present judgment is. You must therefore, at present, confide in the counsels of prudent and discreet advisers, who now judge as you will yourself, when you have attained their age and experience.

CHAP. IV.

IMITATION TO BE FEARED.

The ignorance of children, in whose minds no strong impressions have yet been made, and in whom no habits have yet been formed, renders them pliable and disposed to imitate every thing they see; it is, for this reason, of the utmost importance to propose to them only good models. None should be suffered to approach them except those whose example is proper to be followed. But as it is impossible that they should not sometimes see, in spite of all the precautions which can be taken, many things which are improper, it is necessary to make them remark, at an early age, the impertinence of certain base and unreasonable persons, whose characters require no respect. We should show them how much these persons are despised, how much they deserve to be so, and how miserable they are, who give themselves up to their passions, and who do not cultivate their reason. You may thus, without accustoming them to mockery, form their taste, and render them sensible to true benevolence. You must not even neglect to open their eyes to certain defects, although in so doing you may expose the weakness of persons they ought to respect; for it cannot be expected, nor is it just to keep children in the dark with regard to the true rules of judging characters. Moreover, the surest method of maintaining them in a correct line of conduct, is to convince them, that it is their bound duty to bear with the defects of others, and to judge no person harshly; that such defects are frequently less than they appear to be, and are often balanced by their good qualities; and that as nothing is perfect on earth, we ought to admire what has the least of imperfection. But although it may be prudent to reserve such instructions as these for extreme cases, we must never fail to instil into their minds true principles, and endeavour to guard them, as much as possible, from imitating the evil exhibited before their eyes. The inclination which children have for imitation, produces a great number of evils especially where they are under the direction of persons who are not governed by principles of virtue, and who do not restrain themselves before them. Almighty God has given to children this pliability, in order that we may the more easily lead them to what is good. Often without speaking to them, we need only show them in others what we wish them to model.

We should also prevent their mimicking ridiculous persons; as this habit of acting like a jester has something in it which is low, and contrary to modesty and quite unbecoming. It is to be feared lest children should acquire this habit, because the warmth of their imaginations, and the pliability of their bodies, joined to their sprightliness, make them easily take all kinds of forms, in order to represent what they see ridiculous. "No foolish jesting" the Scripture warns. It is in childhood that the spirit learns to laugh appropriately with those who laugh, and weep with those who weep; everything in its time, where proper speech accompanies proper conduct. In order to avoid being austere and forbidding, however, we must give our children a freedom to express joy and exultation. Life is to be celebrated and enjoyed. Every breath is a gift; every sunset is a reminder of the beauty of life.

CHAP. V.

INDIRECT INSTRUCTION—
GENTLE MEANS.

It has always been my opinion that indirect modes of communicating instructions are much less tiresome to children than lessons and reprimands. They not only awaken their attention to the examples which we would wish to give them but calms the spirit which assists the mind in understanding.

Those who govern children without pretense will find children are much more transparent than people imagine; and from the moment they perceive any duplicity or unregulated authority in those who govern them, they lose that simplicity and confidence so natural to them.

The mind of a child is soft and pliable which allows easy impressions upon it; we should therefore lose no time to imprint on their minds those characters which are so easily formed there. But we must choose images which we would wish to impress upon them; for in so small and so precious a reservoir, we should lay up no froth but exquisite things.

It is to be remembered that we should throw nothing into the minds, at this tender age, but what we would desire to remain there during life. The first images engraved on the mind, while the brain is yet impressionable, and before any thing else is written there, are far the most durable. They harden in proportion as age dries the brain; thus they become at last indelible; hence it is for this reason that we so distinctly recollect, when we are old, the things which have happened to us in our youth, however distant the period may be, rather than those which have happened in a more advanced age; because the traces of these were made in the brain when it was already dry, and full of other images.

When we hear this reasoning, we are inclined to think that it is not just. It is, nevertheless, true, that we reason thus without being aware of it. Do we not say to ourselves every day: My character is formed; I am too old to change; I was brought up in this way of thinking? Besides, do we not feel a particular pleasure in recalling to our minds the images of our youth? Are not our strongest inclinations those which we imbibed at that age? Does not all this prove that the first impressions and habits are the strongest? If then infancy be the time to impress images on the brain, it must be acknowledged that it is not the best for reasoning.

The brain of a child is like a lighted taper exposed to the wind, being always glimmering. The child puts a question to you, and before you have answered it, his eyes are raised towards the ceiling, he counts all the figures which are painted there, or all the panes of glass in the window: if you would drive him back to his first object, you restrain him as if you were to imprison him. You must not, therefore, strain such delicate organs but manage with great care and patience, whilst they are acquiring strength: answer quickly and shortly his questions, and leave him to ask others according to his inclination. Satisfy his curiosity, and let the memory amass for itself a store of good materials. The time will come when he will assemble them; his brain having more consistency, he will be able to follow a continued reasoning. You must forbear to correct him though he should not reason justly; and you should make him feel, without eagerness, as he may give you occasion, how to draw a right inference.

Suffer then a child to play, mixing instruction with amusement: let wisdom appear to him at intervals, and always with a smiling face. Be careful not to fatigue him by an indiscreet exactness.

If a child take up a dark and sullen view of virtue; if independence and vice assume an attractive aspect, all is lost; your work is vain; never suffer him to be flattered by persons of little understanding, or of irregular conduct. We should accustom ourselves to love the manners and the sentiments of those whom we esteem; the pleasure which we at first experience from persons of ill conduct, makes us, by little and little, come to esteem that which is to be despised.

To make children enamoured with virtuous characters, point out to them their sincerity, their modesty, their disinterestedness, their fidelity, and their discretion; but, above all, their piety, which is the genuine source of every virtuous qualification.

If another child of exemplary piety, display some defect in character, say that these defects do not originate in virtue; we all come forth from the womb speaking lies and it is only by the Spirit's help that we overcome our flawed character. Children who understand their own weaknesses will develop a forbearing spirit and a merciful heart. Though you may even watch over yourself, that nothing may be seen in you but what is good, yet you must not expect the child will never find any fault in you; he will frequently find out even your lightest faults. We should therefore model forgiveness, mercy, and forbearance to children, as our heavenly Father has extended these gifts to those of us.

Augustine tells us, that even in his infancy he noticed the vanity of his masters. It is most important that you should know your own faults, which the child will very soon discover in you; welcome the admonitions of some charitable friend, to point out those defects, which you yourself cannot see. Generally, those who govern children pardon nothing in them, though they pardon every thing in themselves. This excites in the children a spirit of criticism and malignity; consequently, when they discover any fault in their governors they are delighted, and feel only contempt for them; this posture of self-righteousness actually creates a vindictive spirit in the child who will glory in such a discovery which furnishes an opportunity for recrimination.

Of all things, avoid this inconvenience; fear not to speak of those defects which are visible in yourself, and of those which may have escaped you in the presence of the child. Be not afraid to acknowledge your evident failings, nor those which inadvertence may have brought to light. If you see him capable of understanding reason on this point, tell him that you will give an example

how to correct his faults, by correcting
your own. Thus, you will draw from your
very imperfections means of instruction
and edification; you will both edify the
child and encourage him to reflect upon
his own faults and correct himself.
Moreover, you will avoid that contempt
and dislike which your defects might
otherwise cause him to feel for your
person.

At the same time, it is necessary to find
out every means of making those things
pleasing to the child which are expected
of him; and should you have any thing
distressing or difficult to propose, forget
not to comfort him with the assurance
that a little trouble will be followed by
unspeakable satisfaction. Always show
him the utility of what you teach, and
the advantages that he will reap in his
future commerce with the world. Make
the usefulness appear with regard to
your commerce, and the respective
duties of your situation. Without these
considerations, study will appear to him
an abstracted labor, barren, thorny, and
full of difficulties. Of what use is it, he
will say to himself, to learn all these

things, of which no one speaks in conversation, and which have nothing to do with daily occupations or any connection with what I have to do? It is therefore necessary to give him a reason and motive for all the things which you teach him. You should say to him: It is to make you more capable of doing what you will have to do one day or other; to form your judgment, and to accustom your mind to reason justly in the different circumstances that may occur to you in life. You should always give to children a solid and agreeable end, that may captivate their young heart, and sweeten their exertions; We should always encourage them in their work, and never pretend to subject them by a dry and absolute authority.

In proportion as their reason augments, it will be well to converse with them more and more on the necessity of their education; not that it should be the means of giving them the power of gratifying all their wishes, but that they should profit by it when they are able to judge of their true state; to exercise their understanding, and to enable them to appreciate justly every thing which it will be necessary for them to do; this then will encourage them to undertake with pleasure tasks for their own improvement.

Never assume, without the greatest necessity, an austere posture, which always frightens children, and often arises from affectation and pedantry in those who govern; for children are generally too timid and bashful. You close their hearts from you by it, and make them withdraw their confidence, without which no good fruit can spring forth, which is necessary to the success of their education. Make yourself beloved by them, and they will be open with you; and they will not fear to let you see their faults. In order to succeed with them, be not too severe with behavior that is not disguised from you. Do not appear astonished or irritated at their bad dispositions; on the contrary, be compassionate to their weaknesses; this inconvenience may arise from too much lenity, and they may be less withheld by fear; but generally approachable confidence and genuineness are more useful to them, than to exercise a rigorous authority over them.

On the other hand, authority will not fail to find its place, if confidence and persuasion are not sufficiently effectual; but you should begin by an open, joyful, and familiar conduct, free from meanness; which gives you the opportunity of seeing children act in their natural state, and of knowing their characters thoroughly. But let not too great familiarity breed contempt. On the other hand, if you should have reduced them by authority to observe all your rules, you would not have gained your end; every thing would become restrained formality, and perhaps hypocrisy. Instead of instilling a love for virtue and knowledge, you will on the contrary give them a general distaste and disgust for both and lose the love of which you should alone seek to inspire them.

If the Wise Man then gave this counsel to parents, to keep the rod always raised above their children; if he said, *that a father who plays with his child shall afterwards weep*, you must not thence conclude that he condemned a patient and gentle education. He only censures those weak and inconsiderate parents, who flatter their children in their passions, and seek merely their own amusement, in indulging them in the most unpardonable excesses. *Editor's note: It appears that there were two wisdom sayings during Fenelon's time:*

- * *"Parents should always keep the rod raised above their children's head."*
- * *"That a father who plays with his child shall afterwards weep."*

These two sayings swing to both sides of the pendulum. On the one hand, you have the authoritative parent who "holds the rod over the child's head" and on the other hand, you have the permissive parent who "plays" and later reaps the consequences. This parent "weeps" in the end. The word "play" is a reference to a parent who acts like a child and allows the child to indulge in all sorts of excesses. This lack of restraint and childish behavior on the part of the parent breeds contempt. It is not the gentle and patient approach to education that is responsible for this breakdown, but solely the lack of character and responsible behavior on the part of the parent or teacher; and though it is essential for parents and teachers to cultivate "friendship" while instructing children, it is equally important that honour is maintained within that relationship. Once this line is crossed, you lose their respect.

The conclusion to be drawn from this is, that parents should always maintain that authority which is necessary for correction; for there are some dispositions which must be governed by fear; but I must repeat, this should only be adopted when no other means will answer.

A child who acts only from the force of his imagination, and who confuses in his mind all the ideas connected with those who present them, will not fail to hate study and virtue, because he is prejudiced against the person who proposes them to him. *Editor's note: I believe Fenelon is saying that children who learn through forceful educational approaches become confused and in the end despise their teachers. Teachers or parents who are harsh and demanding breed disgust for the subject they are trying to teach. This should particularly be emphasized when preparing to teach the Scriptures.*

From this proceeds that idea of piety, so dismal and so frightful, which is frequently retained during life: often this is the whole that he retains of a severe education.

It is frequently necessary to tolerate things which ought to be corrected, until the moment shall have arrived when the mind of the child will be in a state to profit by the correction. Never find fault with him in his first emotion, or in yours; if you do it in yours, he will perceive that you are governed by mood and impatience, and not by reason and friendship: you will lose, without resource, your authority. If you reprimand him in his first emotion, his mind will not be sufficiently free to acknowledge his fault, to subdue his passion, and to weigh the importance of your advice. It is even exposing the child to lose the respect he owes you. Show him always that you have command over yourself, always calm and considerate; nothing will make him see it better than your patience. Watch for a fit moment for several successive days, if necessary, that you may properly time a correction. Do not tell the child his fault, without adding some means by which he may get the better of it, which will encourage him to do so; for we should avoid the discouragement which arises from dry correction. If we find a child somewhat reasonable, I believe it may be well to encourage him gently to ask us to point out his faults; this is a means of pointing them out without giving him pain; and we should never tell him many at a time.

It is not to be forgotten that children have weak heads; that their age renders them yet sensible only to pleasure; and that we often demand from them an exactitude and seriousness of which even we ourselves are incapable. We make even a dangerous impression of weariness and sadness on their temperament, by speaking to them always of words and of things which they cannot comprehend; they are incessantly bored, deprived of moderate liberty and enjoyment, kept always at their books, and in profound silence, tormented with forced postures, with corrections and threats, that serve only to stupify and disgust them.

The ancients understood the treatment of children much better, particularly the method of communicating instruction. It was by the pleasures of poetry and music, that the principle sciences, the maxims of virtue, politeness and good manners were introduced among the Hebrews, Egyptians, and Greeks. Those who are not well read, will scarcely believe this; it is totally contrary to our customs; but whoever has even a slight knowledge of ancient history, will know that this was the common practise for many ages. Let us, however, confine ourselves to our own customs, in order to join the agreeable with the useful as much as we can. But though we can hardly hope to succeed always without employing fear with ordinary children, whose dispositions are stubborn and untractable, we must not have recourse to it till we have patiently tried the effects of milder remedies. We should be ever careful to make them clearly comprehend what we require of them, and with what we shall be content; for if you do not inspire them with an habitual joy and confidence, their minds will become clouded, and their courage will fail; if they are of a lively disposition, we irritate them; if they are gentle, we render them stupid. Fear is like those violent remedies which we employ in the most severe cases of disease; they purge it is true, but they alter the temperament, and exhaust the organs. The mind led by fear becomes always weaker and the heart harder.

Moreover, although we must not always threaten without punishing, we must chastise less frequently than we threaten, lest we give them a contempt for our menaces. As for chastisement, the pain should be as light as possible, but accompanied by all the circumstances which may affect the child with shame and remorse. For example, show him all you have done to avoid this extremity; appear afflicted by it; speak before him to others of the misfortune of those who are void both of reason and honour, and the necessity to chastise such disreputable base characters. *Editor's note: Fenelon is not saying to speak about the child before others, but to allow him to hear your conversations when you speak about others who lack reason and honour; and of course without gossip or slander.* Withdraw from him your usual marks of friendship, until you see that he has need of consolation; make this chastisement according as you shall judge it most useful to the child, either to cause him a great degree of shame, or to show him that you will spare him from it. Make use sometimes of a reasonable person to console the child, who may say to him what you could not then say yourself; who will relieve him from his false shame, who will dispose him to return to you, and to whom the child, in his first emotion, can open his heart more freely than he would be able to do to you. But above all things, do not let it appear to the child that you demand from him unnecessary submissions; endeavour to influence him to condemn himself, that he may submit with a good grace, and that it may only remain with you to soften the pain which he has accepted. *Editor's note: The softening of the "pain" is in reference to "pain" of humility or a change in attitude that brings a child to a place of obedient submission. It is during this time that the parent needs to console and comfort, thus "softening the pain." God modeled this approach throughout the biblical record when His people repented.* Every one must employ these general rules according to the particular occasions. Men, and still less children, do not always resemble themselves; what is commendable to-day may be improper to-morrow; and invariably uniform conduct may not be sometimes useful. *Editor's note: Acceptable behavior for one child may be different for another depending upon maturity, mental health, culture, and socio-economic backgrounds. Though it is our goal to bring children to similar levels of obedient and loving submission, it is equally important to approach each child in accordance to their individual needs, sensitivities, and maturity level. Again, God approaches us as individuals.* The less we give children of set lessons, the better; an infinite variety of instructions more useful than lessons may be conveyed in cheerful and casual conversations. I have known many children who learned a good deal whilst they were at play; this is done by recounting to them some entertaining matter which we take from a book in their presence, and by teaching them insensibly their lessons. After this, they will of themselves desire to find the source of that which gives them so much pleasure.

There are two common errors in the education of children which generally prevents their progress: *first*, when we make them begin to learn to read Latin at an early age, which takes away all the pleasure of reading; and, *secondly*, when we accustom them to read with an affected and ridiculous emphasis. We should give them books well ornamented, even on the outside, with the most beautiful pictures, and characters well formed; every thing which pleases the imagination facilitates study! We should endeavour to choose books full of short and wonderful histories; this done, be not in trouble about the child's learning to read correctly. Let him pronounce naturally as he speaks: when his tongue shall be pliable, and his lungs stronger, and the habit of reading greater, he will read without difficulty, more gracefully and more distinctly.

The manner of teaching to write ought to be nearly the same. When a child already knows how to read a little, we may make it a diversion for him to form letters; and if there are many together, you may cause an emulation amongst them. Children of their own accord will apply themselves to make figures on paper; if we assist this inclination a little, without restraining them too much, they will form letters as they play, and accustom themselves by degrees to write. We may even excite them by promising them some recompense which will be to their taste, but which will not have any dangerous consequence.

Write me a note, you may say to the child; ask something for your brother or your cousin; all this gives pleasure to the child, provided no dull images or regulated lessons be found in it to trouble him. An unrestrained curiosity, says Augustine from his own personal experience, acts more powerfully on the minds of youth, than rules and necessities imposed through fear.

Let us here remark a great defect in the common modes of education. We put all the pleasure on one side, and all the weariness on the other. The weariness on that of study, the pleasure on that of diversion. What can a child do, but impatiently support the drudgery of learning, and run ardently after play?

Let us then endeavour to change this order; let us render study pleasing; let us conceal the trouble under the appearance of liberty and delight. Let us suffer the children to interrupt their study by little sallies of diversion; these distractions are necessary, and ought therefore to be allowed, purposely to refresh their minds, that are so easily fatigued even by a short application.

Suffer them to walk about a little; permit them even now and then, some digression, or some play, that will unbend their minds; then bring them back gently to the task. Too much regularity in exacting from them an uninterrupted application to study, hurts them too much; those who govern often affect this regularity, because it is more convenient to themselves, than subjecting themselves continually to the proper moments of instruction.

At the same time, we must take from children all those diversions which too much inflame their passions; and to introduce in its stead an agreeable variety of innocent diversions that can refresh their mind, that can satisfy their curiosity for useful things, that can exercise their bodies to agreeable arts; all these should be employed in the diversions of children. What they value the most, is what keeps their bodies in the most constant motion; they are content, provided they often change their position; a shuttlecock or a ball is sufficient. Thus, there is no necessity of racking the brain to invent new playthings, they will invent new ones themselves; all that is required is to permit them to act, to observe them with a joyful countenance, and to moderate them as soon as they become overheated.

It is good simply to make them feel, as much as possible, the pleasures which the mind derives from conversation, from mental amusements, news, anecdotes, and history; especially from the several historical accounts of ingenuity, which convey instruction. All this will one day or other turn to profit; but the inclination of children must not be forced; we should only offer the opportunity to him to exercise it; teach during moments of lively conversation. All this must be used according to the occasion; some days the body will be less disposed to move about, and the mind will be more active.

The care which we should take to season serious occupations with pleasure, will serve much to abate the ardor of youth for dangerous pleasures. *Editor's note: Christians who love what they do generally live life with confidence and purpose and have little time for irrational and harmful activities. It was Mary Luaretta who said, "To be successful, the first thing to do is fall in love with your work."* It is subjection and weariness which give such an impatient desire for diversion. If a child felt less tired in the company of his mother or governess, he would not wish so much to escape from her, to seek other company perhaps not so good for him.

In the choice of diversions, all dangerous connections should be avoided. Boys are not to be permitted to play with girls indiscriminately, and the girls must only choose for their comrades or companions such as are orderly and unobjectionable. Activities which dissipate, and which excite passion too much, or which occasion an unbecoming exertion of the body, which would not be modest, should be carefully avoided. A young lady or young man can easily find wherewith to amuse themselves, unless some ardent diversion, have corrupted their taste. Health and innocence are the true sources of enjoyment; but those who have had the misfortune to accustom themselves to violent pleasures, lose all taste for those of a more moderate nature, and fatigue themselves in a restless pursuit, seeking after excessive gratifications.

We spoil our taste for simple pleasures as we do for ordinary cuisine; we accustom ourselves to high-flavored dishes, till those which are simple and unseasoned become flat and insipid. Let us then fear those great emotions of the mind which lead to weariness and disgust; but above all, they are to be feared for those children who never resist their feelings, and who are always seeking emotion. Let us give them a taste for simple things, to the end that simple amusements may content their palate. A simple walk through the woods or splashing in a stream brings contentment to the soul and appreciation for God's beauty in a manner that extravagant amusements cannot. Moderation is the best sauce; it gives sufficient appetite, requires no high seasoning, and is a stranger to intemperance. Moderation, said an ancient writer, is the parent of pleasure. With this moderation, which produces health of body and mind, we can maintain an undisturbed and rational enjoyment. We neither require public shows, nor require a great expense to enjoy ourselves; a little play which we invent, reading a good book, some work which we undertake, the most exquisite music, a walk for amusement, an innocent conversation which refreshes after labor, makes us feel a purer joy than extravagant activities.

These simple amusements are certainly less lively and less affecting; others agitate more forcibly the soul, in touching the strings of the passions; but plain and simple pleasures are preferable, as they afford an equal and lasting enjoyment, without leaving any hurtful impression. They are always beneficial, whilst the others resemble adulterated wine, which pleases, at first the palate, but in the end prejudices the health. Thus the temper of mind, not less than the natural appetite, can be spoiled by elaborate gratification of the senses. It is of the utmost importance that we bring children up to a plain way of life, to strengthen in them this excellent habit, and give them a true insight into the dreadful inconveniencies concomitant on other pleasures, and not to abandon them to themselves, as is generally the case, at an age when the passions are most restless, and of course, when they stand most in need of a discreet moderator.

Of all the troubles of education, none are to be compared to that of bringing up a child who lacks sensibility and shews no disposition for improvement. Children with lively dispositions are capable of great wanderings. Passion and presumption lead them on but they often return from error. Instruction in them is like a seed committed to the ground, which shoots up and fructifies, specially when experience comes to the assistance of reason, and when the passions cool: at least, we know how to recall their attention, to excite their curiosity. We have in them, incentives, that will touch them; we can by means of their sense of honour and disgrace, prompt them to take an interest in the instructions given them; whereas in slothful children, we have no power whatever to raise their inactivity, to call forth their latent talents. All the thoughts of such are distracting, they never are where they ought to be; you cannot even move them much by correction; they hear all, but feel nothing. Children of this character are always negligent, and disgusted with what they undertake; and here the very best education is in danger of failing, if we do not endeavour from the first dawn of reason to remedy the evil.

Many persons who do not reflect deeply, conclude from this ill success, that every thing depends on nature in forming the man of merit, and that education has nothing to do in it; whilst, on the contrary, they ought only to conclude that there are some dispositions, like some ungrateful soils, on which the greatest efforts of cultivation are apparently lost. But it is infinitely worse, when the education of these ungrateful dispositions is either neglected, or ill managed in the beginning.

It is also to be observed, that there are children in whose dispositions we are greatly deceived. They appear at first lovely, and witty, and captivating, because there is something so charming and fascinating in the first graces of a child, that every defect is thereby concealed. We expect but little at that age; hence, every attempt at wit arrests our astonishment: all faults of judgment are overlooked. It is here in infancy that seems to promise so much, and gives so little. Such a one has been celebrated for his wit until the age of five years, but afterwards has fallen into obscurity and contempt in proportion as he grew up. Of all the qualities which we see in children, there is only one on which we can depend—it is the faculty of reasoning; it grows always with them, provided it be well cultivated. The graces of infancy wear out, vivacity extinguishes itself, tenderness of heart is even sometimes lost, the charms of youth disappear, because their passions overcome their sensibilities as they embark upon the wide ocean of the world, where dangerous discussions with men insensibly harden their hearts. Endeavour then to discover, through the graces of youth, if the dispositions of the child entrusted to your charge be devoid of sensible emulation. In this case, it will be difficult for those charged with his education not to be soon repulsed by a labor so ungrateful and thorny. Here it is necessary to stir up all the resources of the soul of the child, to draw him out of his lethargy. If you foresee this inconvenience, this sluggishness of disposition, do not at first overburden his memory with long tasks and repeated instructions; take great care not to overcharge his memory, for it is this which stuns and weighs down the brain. Oppress him not with hard rules, but endeavour to inspirit him. Do not fear to show him, with discretion, of what he is capable; content yourself with little, make him remark his most trifling success; represent to him how unfounded were his fears that he would not succeed in what he had done well. Let not emulation, that strong incentive to bold undertakings, lie dormant. Jealousy is a passion far stronger in children that we have any conception of; we see them sometimes, from it, shutting up their minds, and wasting with some secret languor, because others are more loved and more admired. It is a cruelty to let them suffer this torment; but cruel as it generally is, we must occasionally know how to avail ourselves of it, as a powerful remedy against slothfulness. Put before your pupil such children only as are possessed with abilities not much above his own level; for if you wish him to rival and emulate others of far superior abilities, the consequence will be, that he will leave his studies more discouraged than ever.

Give him, from time to time, little victories over those with whom he is jealous; engage him, if you can, to join with you in laughing freely with you at his own reluctance and timidity; show him others like himself, who got the better of this defect of their constitution; teach him, by indirect instructions, addressed to a third person, that timidity and idleness stifle the spirit and are enemies to the powers of the mind; that persons who are lazy, and without application, whatever genius they may have, become imbecile and degraded; but take good care not to give these instructions in an austere or impatient tone, for nothing so much shuts up the mind of a child, who is dull and timid, as harshness: on the contrary, redouble your care to season, and to make the labor which you cannot spare him, easy and pleasant, in proportion to his natural disposition; make explanations simple and easy to understand, with the necessary amusements proportioned to his genius and abilities. Perhaps it will be necessary, from time to time, to spur him forward, by reflecting on his little progress. You must not do it yourself; but some one inferior, as another child, may do it without your appearing to know it.

Augustine relates, that a well-timed reproach made to Monica, his mother, in her youth, by a servant, affected her so much as to induce her to leave off a bad habit which she had acquired, of drinking pure wine, *i.e.* wine not diluted with water: which the vehemence and severity of her governess had not the power of doing. In short, we must endeavour to give taste to the minds of children of this disposition, as you would to sick persons that have no appetite. We suffer them to seek whatever may cure their incapacities; You may even indulge them in certain eccentricities, contrary to normal circumstances, provided they do not go to any dangerous excess. It is more difficult to give taste to those who have it not, than to form that of those who have not already such as it ought to be. *Editor's note: parents and teachers need to creatively explore educational opportunities that will excite and enliven the passions of children. It is far more important that a child learn one thing well while enjoying the process of learning, than many things poorly with ill will.*

Another kind of sensibility, still more difficult and more important, which you will have to form in your young pupils; I mean that of friendship. As soon as your little charge is capable of it, your whole business will be, to give his tender heart a proper inclination and affection to those persons that may be useful to her*. Friendship of itself will have power to accomplish almost any thing you can wish; and if it be discreetly managed, it

---

More may be learned from the conversation of a discreet, virtuous, and experienced friend, than from any instruction communicated by books or dry lessons: if the latter enrich, the former polishes the mind.

will serve you as a chain to draw him
without restraint to the practise of virtue
and of all good, provided we know how to
make use of it. Excess, or a bad choice in
his affections, is the only rock you can
have to fear or avoid. It must, however,
be confessed, that this amiability of
disposition is not found in all children.
There are some children who are born
politicians, shrewd, and with an
apparent indifference, yet desirous to
draw every thing secretly to themselves;
they deceive their parents, whom
tenderness renders credulous; they
pretend to love them; they study their
inclinations in order to conform to them;
they appear more docile than other
children of the same age, who act
without disguise according to their mood;
their subtlety, which hides their self-will,
a cloak for their sour temper, appears to
be nothing but gentleness and
sweetness, and their natural turn of
mind does not wholly display itself, till
there is no longer time to redress it.

If there be children upon whose
dispositions education can do nothing, it
is beyond all doubt, that which we have

just mentioned; and their number, I am sorry to add, is infinitely greater than many are willing to imagine. The fondness of parents for their offspring, makes them very unwilling to believe that their children have bad hearts; and when they will not see it with their own eyes, no one likes to undertake to point it out to them, and the evil every day grows more obstinate and more incurable.

The first and best preventative is, to allow children, in their earliest infancy, whilst free from guile and artifice, to discover their true character and turn of mind. Parents must know their children thoroughly, before they attempt to correct them. Of their own nature, children are open, candid, and undisguised; but if you torment them, or shew them the least example of disguise or concealment, they never more return to their native simplicity. Sensibility and sweetness of temper are certainly gifts of Almighty God. We can only endeavour to excite it by noble and generous examples, by honorable maxims, by kindness, and by showing contempt for those people who have too much self-love. It is necessary to make children taste, at an early age, before they have lost their first simplicity, by emotions the most natural, the pleasure of a cordial and reciprocal friendship. Nothing will answer this purpose so well, as to place persons who never show any harsh, false, or low treatment, near them. It would be better to place about them those who have other faults, but who are exempt from these. We should also praise children for every thing which they do from friendship, provided it be not out of place, or too ardent. They must also be able to observe in their parents a true and sincere friendship for them; for children often learn, even from their parents, to shew no affection to any persons whatever. In short, I would withhold from them, with regard to friends, all superfluous compliments, all pretended demonstrations of regard, and all false caresses, by which we may teach them to make vain appearance towards persons whom they ought to love. *Editor's note: Parents who allow their children to bask in the shallow praise and false admiration of either themselves or others, risk having their children imitate the same vain expressions.*

There is another fault the opposite to this which we have represented, that is more common amongst girls. It is that of being passionately fond of even the most indifferent things or persons. They cannot see two persons who differ with one another, without taking part in their hearts for one side or the other; they are full of affection, or aversion, but without the least foundation or motive. In persons they esteem and admire, they can discern no imperfections, and no good quality in those whom they dislike. It would not be prudent to oppose them abruptly; in this case, opposition might only rivet and confirm their fancies: but, we must endeavour to convince young people by degrees, that we are better able to judge of what there is, either charming or displeasing, in the person she so much admires. Do not fail, as occasion offers, to let her feel the inconveniencies that arise from the defect of the person she judged faultless, and of the advantages that are derived from the good qualifications of the person she so unjustly slighted. Do not press the subject too much, for you will soon see that they will return to themselves. After this, let her pass in review her former excitement, or fits of passion and folly, with all their unreasonable circumstances, and tell her quietly, that the time will most undoubtedly arrive when she will form the same judgment of her other little follies, which she has not as yet learned how to subdue. Relate to them of the same errors of which you were guilty at their age. Above all, make her as sensible as you possibly can of the great mixture of good and evil that is invariably found in whatever we love or hate in this world, and this purposely to dampen the excessive passion of her affections and disgusts.

Never promise to give children, as a recompense, either articles of dress or delicacies: for this would be causing two evils; the first by inspiring them with an esteem for what they ought to despise, and secondly, it would be losing the favourable opportunity of establishing other rewards, that might greatly facilitate your future instructions. Take good care never to threaten them with any thing to study, nor to subject them to various rules. We should make as few rules as possible, unless they cannot be avoided, endeavouring to bring it about quietly, without forceful necessity; we should always shew some sufficient reason for doing the task at this time, and in this place, rather than in another. We run the risk of discouraging children, if we never praise them when they do well. Though praises are to be feared on account of vanity, still we must endeavour to make use of them to encourage children, without flattering them. Well-timed praise may be profitably used as a stimulus to industry, but not as an incitement to intoxicating self-esteem.

We observe that St. Paul employs praises often to encourage the weak, and to soften correction. It is true, that in order to render them useful, we must adapt them so as to take from them all appearance of exaggeration or flattery, and, at the same time, attribute all the good to God as its true source. We can also reward children by permitting them to play at innocent games which require some skill and ingenuity; by walks, in which instructive conversation may be introduced; by little presents, which will be a sort of prize; such as prints, pictures, medals, maps, or ornamented books.

CHAP. VI.

ON THE ADVANTAGES OF HISTORY FOR CHILDREN.

Children are passionately fond of wonderful and illustrative tales; we see them continually transported with joy, or shedding tears, at the recital of adventures which we relate to them. Do not fail to profit by this inclination. When you see them disposed to hear you, recount to them some short and meaningful story, which will be ingenious and innocent; children young and old love stories, especially fables. As to heathen fables, it is better that children should be always ignorant of them, because, generally speaking, they are impure, and full of impious absurdities. If you cannot keep them entirely ignorant of them, inspire, as much as possible, a horror of them. When you shall have recounted one story, wait till the child of her own accord, solicits you to tell more; his thirst for them being thus awakened, and his curiosity is wound up to its proper pitch, relate certain select histories, but in a few words; connect them together, and put off from day to day the relation of the sequel, in order to hold the child in suspense, and to give him an impatience to know the end; animate your recitals with a lively and familiar tone; make all your characters speak. Children who have lively imaginations will believe that they see and hear what you tell them. For example, relate the beautiful and interesting history of Joseph to them; make his brothers speak like savages, Jacob as an affectionate and afflicted father; when Joseph himself speaks, let him take pleasure in being master in Egypt, in keeping himself unknown to his brothers, to excite their fear, and then finally to discover himself. This natural and simple representation, joined to the marvelousness of the history, will charm the child beyond expression: provided we do not overload him with such recitals, and that we leave him free to wish for them; that we promise them even as a recompense when he behaves well; that we do not give them as lessons, nor oblige the child to repeat them. To desire of him to repeat these stories, unless he shew a desire of his own accord, would lay him under an unpleasant restraint, and would greatly take away from the satisfaction. *Editor's note: The question of age is important here. Fenelon's advice appears to be best suited for children in the early elementary years. Though teachers in the higher grades should expect students to memorize important historical facts, it is essential that the material is presented in story form, raising the same degree of suspense and interest as prescribed for younger children. Why should we resort to dry and boring lectures that serves little to excite the passions or love for learning? Older students need to be engaged to think and ask questions. Take them back in time to feel the tensions of great historical episodes, and involve them in all the emotional decisions that are still talked about hundreds of years later. In contrast to tests that measure only an ability to memorize lists, focus more on the retelling of the histories in relation to the circumstances of the past and the present. Once a student is able to retell the history in his own account, he will remember much more relevant information than the traditional exams of fill in the blank, true and false, and multiple choice. Teachers teach facts but educators engage students in thinking; and thinking requires students to ask questions. Students who are fearful of missing facts for an upcoming exam, rarely have time to think critically. Critical thinking is best enriched in a relaxed atmosphere, where dialogue and discussion are encouraged.*

We should, nevertheless, observe whether, if the child has any facility in expressing himself, he will naturally and on his own accord relate, to some person whom he loves, the histories which have given him most pleasure; you can make use of some person who is very free with the child, and who may appear to desire to learn the story from him; he will in those circumstances be happy to tell it. Do not appear to pay any attention; let him do it without being reminded of his faults. *Editor's note: In the early years of education it is imperative that children are not discouraged with repeated corrections and low grades. It is the responsibility of parents and teachers to help children to succeed and gain confidence in their ability to think and learn. If a child is not lazy, and is working hard, though not able to grasp the content, this child should never lose privileges or be made to feel that he is a failure. On the contrary, this child should be rewarded for his effort.*

Then, when he has acquired a habit of retelling a story, you may then let him see what is the best method of relating any fact. This is, to tell it in as short, simple, and natural a manner as possible, and to select those circumstances in preference, which are most intimately connected with the subject, and which represent to life the nature of the fact. If you have many children to instruct, accustom them by degrees to represent the characters of the histories which they have learned; let them each have a part to act; the one will be Abraham, the other Isaac. These representations will charm them more than any diversion; they will accustom them to think and to speak of serious subjects with pleasure, and will render these histories indelibly fixed in their memories. *Editor's note: There are three books that are written with such descriptive language and beauty that the historical accounts will indeed be indelibly fixed upon the child's mind. The titles are: "The Pillar of Fire" by J.H. Ingraham, "Titus: A Comrade of the Cross" by F.M. Kingsley, and "Joel: A Boy of Galilee" by Annie Fellows Johnston. See appendix for further recommendations.*

We should endeavour to give them more taste for sacred history than for any other, not by telling them that these are prettier, which probably they would not perhaps believe, but by making them feel it without telling them. Point out to them how very important, singular and marvellous they are, how full of exquisite and natural pictures, and with what simplicity, dignity and vivacity, they are related. Those of the creation, of the fall of Adam, of the deluge, of the call of

Abraham, of the sacrifice of Isaac, of the adventures of Joseph which we have mentioned, of the birth and the flight of Moses, are subjects not only calculated to rouze children's curiosity, but moreover to fix the principles of the *Sacred Writ* in their minds by exposing its origin. We must be grossly ignorant of the essential foundation of religion in relation to education, not to see that it is all historical; for it is by a chain of extraordinary facts, that we find its establishment, its perpetuity, and every thing which ought to make us believe and practise it.

We are not to imagine that we shall be able to engage young persons to dive deeply into this science, when we propose to them all these histories, even though they are short, varied, and adapted to please the most ignorant. Almighty God, who knows better than we do the mind of man which he has formed, has put the Sacred Writings into resplendent and popular facts, which, so far from overcharging the weakest minds, on the contrary assist them to conceive and to retain its mysteries. For example, say to a child, that in God three equal persons are but one single nature. In consequence of hearing and repeating these terms, he will retain them in his memory; but I doubt whether he will be able to conceive the sense of them. Relate to him that when Jesus Christ was coming out of the waters of Jordan, his Father caused his voice to be heard from heaven, saying: "This is my beloved Son, in whom I am well pleased; hear ye him." Add, that the Holy Ghost descended on him in the form of a dove, and in this little history you will give him an idea of the Trinity that will never escape her. Behold here three persons, whom he will always distinguish by the difference of their actions; you will only have to teach him, that altogether they are but one God. This example is sufficient to show the utility of such facts; though they appear to lengthen the instruction, they shorten it much, and take from it the dullness of catechisms, in which the mysteries are detached from the facts. Let us see if the ancients instructed by this means. The admirable manner in which Augustine advises the ignorant to be instructed, was not a method which he introduced; it was the universal method and practise of the early church. It consisted in showing, by the succession of history, that religion was as ancient as the world; that Jesus Christ, the promised Messiah, was expected in the Old Testament, but manifested in the New Testament. This is the abridgment of the whole christian faith.

This demands a little more time and care than the instruction to which most persons confine themselves; but then we know the teachings of the God of all creation truly, when we know these details; on the contrary, when we are ignorant of them, we have but confused ideas of Jesus Christ, of the gospel, and the foundation of those virtues with which the christian doctrine ought to inspire us.

Let us then join to the histories which I have remarked, the passage of the Red Sea, and the sojourn of the people in the desert, where they ate bread which fell from heaven, and drank of water which Moses drew from a rock, by striking it with his rod. Represent the miraculous conquest of the promised land, when the waters of the Jordan returned towards their source, and the walls of a city fell of themselves at the sight of the besiegers. Figure to them in the most natural colours, the battles between Saul and of David. Show how David, from his youth, without arms, in his shepherd's dress, vanquished the fierce giant, Goliath. Do not forget the glory and the wisdom of Solomon; make him decide between the two women who disputed about the child; but show him falling from the height of his wisdom, and dishonoring himself by sensual indulgence, a consequence almost inevitable of too much prosperity.

Make the prophets speak to the kings on the part of God; introduce them describing things to come, with the same precision, as if the events had already taken place, and had been consigned to the faithful page of history. Represent the prophets as men of the most exemplary and contrite lives; let them appear humble, austere, and suffering continual persecutions for having told the truth. Shew them in proper succession the first ruin of Jerusalem; show the burning of the temple reduced to ashes, and the holy city levelled to the ground on account of the crying sins of the people. Recount the captivity of Babylon, where the Jews wept for their beloved Zion. Before their return, introduce the delightful adventures of Shadrach, Meshach, Abednego, Esther, Ruth, and Daniel. It would not be useless to make the children give an opinion on the different characters of these saints, to discover those whom they admire most. One will prefer Esther, another Ruth, and this will excite a little contention between them, which will impress the history more strongly on their minds, and form their judgment. Then lead back the people to Jerusalem, make them repair its ruin; make a smiling picture of peace, and of its happiness; soon after, draw a portrait of the cruel and impious Antiochus, who died calling for mercy, but in vain. Show, under this persecution, the victories of the Macabees, and the martyrdom of the seven brothers of that name. Come to the

miraculous birth of John the Baptist.
Relate, in more detail, that of Jesus
Christ; you must then choose in the
gospel history the most remarkable
circumstance of his life—his preaching in
the temple at the age of twelve years—
his baptism—his retreat to the desert,
and his temptation—the vocation of his
apostles—the miracle of the loaves—the
conversation of the sinful woman who
anointed the feet of our Saviour with the
perfumed ointment, washed them with
her tears, and dried them with her hair.
Represent moreover, the instruction of
the Syrophoenecian woman, the cure of
the man born blind, Lazarus restored to
life, and Jesus Christ triumphantly
riding into Jerusalem. Let them notice
his passion, and describe him gloriously
rising from the tomb. Make them remark
the familiar manner in which he
remained forty days with his disciples,
until they saw him ascend into heaven,
conferring the blessing, saying, "Lo, I am
with you always, even till the end of the
age." You must next mention in order the
descent of the Holy Spirit in cloven
tongues of fire, the stoning of Stephen,

the conversion of Paul, and the call to the centurion Cornelius. The different journies of the apostles both by land and sea, particularly of Paul, will (if you take the pains to point out the track and the different places mentioned on a map) afford great satisfaction. Make a choice of the most marvellous histories of the martyrs, and something of the committed lives of the first Christians; mix here the courage of the young virgins, the astonishing sobriety of the early church fathers, the conversion of emperors, and then of the whole empire; the blindness of the Jews, and their terrible punishment, which continues till this day.

All these accounts, managed discreetly, will be received with pleasure into the imaginations of lively and tender children. The whole course of religion, from the creation of the world to the present time, gives noble ideas to them, which will never be forgotten. They will even see, in this history, the hand of God always raised to deliver the just, and to confound the impious; on the other hand, they will also see that God's people do suffer for righteousness and at times the wicked do prosper; but in all of history and at all times, God intends for good what others have intended for evil. They will be accustomed to see God, the author of every thing, working, by ways only known to himself, his grand design for each of our lives, though at times hard to understand. It is with this truth in mind, that children learn to trust in him who is invisible yet upholds with an outstretched and secure arm –for he will never leave us nor forsake us. Moreover, they shall see even the very persons who appear the most wicked, bring to fulfillment the very will of God; one would not have to search long to find these connexions.

In these different histories care must be taken to select the most smiling and magnificent images, because every opportunity must be used to make our christian doctrine appear beautiful, lovely and sublime; whereas persons in the world are too apt to look upon religion as is generally the case, melancholy and disgusting.

Besides the inestimable advantage of thus teaching religion to children by this method, this stock of interesting stories, which have been entrusted to their memory when very young, will, as they grow up, naturally excite their curiosity for serious matters of the imagination, renders them sensible to the pleasures of the mind, and will make them take an interest in other histories, that may have some connexion and analogy with the stories they already possess. I must, however, repeat that it is necessary to guard against making it a law for them to hear, or be obliged to remember these stories, much less to make them regular lessons. Pleasure of itself must do the business; for true education emerges from the bowels of pleasure and a love for learning. Do not press them; you will obtain your end even with the slowest capacities; avoid overcharging their memory, and their curiosity will increase with age.

But you will say, how are we to relate these histories in a lively—short— natural, and agreeable manner? Where can we find governesses equal to the task?—My answer is, that I merely propose this plan, to encourage parents to be persevering, to find persons of good minds and pure hearts, to govern children, and that we should inspire them as much as possible to maintain virtue, honour, and humility; and let them be pressingly admonished and solicited to follow, as near as they can, the method I have here laid down before them. For, if governesses, possessed of very moderate abilities, will only form themselves upon this model, the education of children will, I am convinced, prove far less defective.

You may add to your discourse the sight of prints or paintings, as well, which agreeably represent the sacred histories. Prints may suffice, and we may generally use them; but when we have the opportunity of showing the children good paintings we should not neglect it; for the force of colors, with the grandeur of figures, will strike their imagination more forcibly.

Together, parent and governess can inspire our young, arouse their curiosities, whet their appetites for further knowledge, and engage them in lively discussions of eternal truths.

CHAP. VII.

How The First Principles Of Christianity May Be Instilled Into Children.

We have remarked, that children in their earliest age are not formed for reasoning. Not that they are without the ideas and general principles of reasoning, which they will finally acquire, but for want of knowing many facts they cannot apply their reason; and on the other hand, the agitation of their brain prevents them from following and connecting their thoughts.

We must, however, without pressing children too much, sweetly convert the first dawn of their reason to the knowledge of God; and gently insinuate into their tender minds a firm conviction of the truths of the Scriptures, without giving them any arguments or motives that may occasion doubt.—For instance, when they see a believing loved one die; they know that he will be buried. Take this opportunity to ask them, if the dead man be in the grave? They will answer, *yes*.—Is he not then gone into heaven? *Yes he is*, they will say.—How then can the dead man be both in the grave and in heaven at the same time? They will answer you; *his soul is gone to heaven, and his body is buried in the grave.*—His soul is not then the body? *No, certainly.*—The soul is not then dead? *No; it will live for ever in heaven.*—You may then add: And as for you, do you wish to be saved? *Yes, most undoubtedly.*—But what do you mean by salvation? *I mean that the soul will ascend to heaven and not to hell when we die.*—And what do you mean by death? *I mean that when the soul quitteth the body, the body dies, and is reduced to its original dust.*—You may then end the discourse by adding: When the soul departs from the body, a believing soul is comforted for ever in the Father's love, and the unbelieving, to the torment of everlasting fire.

I do not pretend that governesses should be obliged to make all their little pupils answer at first in this manner;

still I can take upon myself to affirm, that several children, not more than four years old, have made me these answers. But on the supposition that there may be some whose geniuses, open later, the only inconvenience will be, that we must wait a few years longer with patience.

We should show children an edifice, and accustom them to learn that this building was not built by itself. The stones, you will tell them, would not have been placed without some person bringing them there. It will be well even to show them some masons who are building: then make them look at the heavens, the earth, and the principle things which God has placed there for man's use and benefit. Then say to them, you see how much more beautiful and better the world is made than any building. And is it possible this world could have made itself? No; certainly; it was the Lord God who built it with his own hands.

Follow at first the precise method of the holy Scriptures; strike their imaginations in a lively manner, and propose nothing to them which is not clothed in images that can reach the senses. Represent God seated on a throne, with eyes more brilliant than the rays of the sun, and more piercing than the most livid lightning. Introduce the Lord as speaking; at one time delivering his holy mandates, at another listening to his people: represent him with hands which carry the universe, arms always raised to punish the wicked, and a heart tender and paternal, always open to receive those who love him. The time will come when you may render all this wisdom more exact. Observe all the openings which the mind of the child gives you; try every means by which these great truths may the better enter his understanding. Above all, tell him nothing new, without familiarizing his mind to it by some easy and sensible comparison.

For example, ask him if he would sooner die than renounce Jesus Christ? He will answer, *yes.* But what, you might add, would you suffer your head to be cut off, to go into heaven? *Yes.* So far the child believes that he should have sufficient courage to make the sacrifice;

but if you wish to make him feel that he can do nothing without the assistance of God's grace, you will gain nothing if you tell him simply that he has need of grace to be faithful; he will not understand the meaning of these words, and if you accustom him to hear them without understanding them, you will not make good your point. What remains to be done? Why, tell him the history of the prince of the apostles, Peter; represent him as saying, in a presumptuous tone: *Though I should die, I will follow thee; and though all others should leave thee, I will never abandon thee.* Then paint to his eyes Peter's disgraceful fall. Three times he denies Jesus Christ; intimidated by a lowly maid-servant. Tell him why God permitted Peter to be so weak; then make use of the comparison of a child, or of a sick person, who cannot stand alone, and make him understand that we have need of God to support us, as a nurse supports a child; by this you will give the child insight into the mystery of grace.

But the truth most difficult to make him understand, is that we have a soul far more precious than our body. The body, they will attend to it but too well; particularly for a girl, every thing conduces to flatter her and induce her to ornament it, and to make it an idol. It is important to inspire her with contempt for it, by showing her that she has something within her of far more worth. Say then to a child, in whom reason begins to act, is it your soul that eats? If she gives a weak answer, do not scold her; but tell her gently that her soul does not eat. It is the body, you will say, that eats, and is like to the beasts. Have the beasts souls? Are they learned? *No,* the child will reply. But they eat, you will continue, though they have no soul. You clearly see, then, that it is not the soul that eats. It is the body which takes food to nourish it. It is the body that walks, and sleeps. And, what does the soul do? It reasons—it knows every body—it has an affection for certain things, and an aversion for others.—Add as it were in play, Do you see this table? *Yes.*—You see well that it is not made like this chair; you know that it is of wood, and that it is not like the chimney, which is of stone? *Yes*, the child will reply. Go no further, unless you see in the tones of his voice and cast of his eyes, that these simple truths have left some sort of impression upon him. Then add, but does this table know you? You will see that he will laugh at the mockery of this question. No matter; ask him, who loves you better: this table, or that chair? He will still laugh. Continue. And the window, is it wise? Then endeavour to advance. And this doll, will it answer when you speak to it? *No*. Why not? Is it because it has no soul? Certainly, it has none. It is not then like you, for you know it, while the doll cannot know you. But, after your death, when you will be in the earth, will you not be like this doll? *Yes*. You will no longer feel or hear any thing? *No*. And your soul will then be in heaven? *Yes*. Will it not see God? *Yes it will*. And the soul of the doll, where is it at present? You will see the child laugh in answering you—but at least you will make him understand that the doll has no soul.

On this foundation, and by these little sensible images, make use of every renewed occasion, to accustom the child by degrees to attribute to the body what belongs to the body and the soul what belongs to the soul; unless you go indiscreetly to work in proposing certain actions that are common both to the soul and body. All subtleties that may confuse these truths should be carefully avoided; and you must content yourself with marking out distinctly those things, where the difference of the body and soul is clearly perceived. Perhaps we may find minds so confined that, even with a good education, they will not be able to understand distinctly these truths; and when we instruct, we may sometimes conceive a thing very clearly, though we do not always know how to explain it well; on the other hand, God sees better than we do, how he has formed the mind of man for the reception of his mysteries.

For those children in whom we perceive talents capable of going farther, we can, without involving them in a philosophical study, make them conceive, according to the capability of their minds, what we mean when we tell them that God is a spirit, and that their soul is also a spirit. I believe that the best and simplest means of making them understand this spirituality of God and of the soul is, to make them remark the difference between a dead and a living man: in the one there is nothing but the body; in the other the body is joined to the soul. Afterward we may show that a being, possessed of reason, is much more perfect than one that is merely capable of motion. Make them also remark, by familiar examples, that nothing perishes. Thus for instance: a piece of wood which is burned becomes ashes. If then you will say, that which is in itself nothing but dust, incapable of knowing and of thinking, never perishes, how much more reason have we to believe that our souls, which know and think, will never cease to exist? The body can die; that is to say, it can quit the soul and become dust, but the soul will live, for it will always think.

Those who teach ought to impress this knowledge as deeply as possible upon the minds of children, for it is the foundation of the most essential truths. For what profit is there, if a man gain the whole world but lose his own soul? And what shall a man give in exchange for his soul? So you can see that this teaching is of the gravest of consequences if not properly taught and thoroughly understood. But when they cannot succeed, they should, instead of being discouraged by their dulness and slow reception, on the contrary, hope and pray that God will enlighten them; for it is God who opens the minds and hearts of all who call upon him; for if you seek him with all your heart, he will let you find him.

There is even a clear and practical way by which this knowledge of the distinction between body and soul may be increased, and this is to accustom the child to despise the one, and to esteem the other, in all the details of morality. Praise those instructions which serve to nurture and improve the soul; and shew your esteem for those grand truths and virtues which animate and inspirit us to the pursuit of piety and true wisdom. On the other hand, let them see that you despise lavish living, immodest and expensive dress, or whatever else may tend to relax one's resolve of mastery over his body; in a word, whatever only softened and degrades the body; that nothing is nearer your heart than solid principles of honour and truth, and a conscious rectitude of conduct, which are enjoyments infinitely superior to the gross and unworthy gratifications of sensual worldlings.

By similar sentiments, without entering on a course of reasoning on the body and the soul, the ancient Romans taught their children, not only to despise their body and make a generous and noble sacrifice of it, but also to indulge and gratify their soul with the delight that is found in virtue and honour. Amongst them not only senators and persons of distinguished birth, but even the plebeians, and the whole of the people were born temperate— disinterested, full of contempt for this life; and they were indifferent with regard to their bodies, but ever feelingly alive to the calls of glory and of wisdom. When I speak of the ancient Romans, I mean those who lived before the power and splendor of their empire had altered the simplicity of their manners.

Let us not say that it would be impossible to give children such a love for honour and virtue by education. How many maxims do we see established amongst ourselves, against the impressions of our feeling, by force of custom? For example, that of *duelling*, founded on a false notion of honour. It is not from reasoning, but from adopting without reasoning, the established maxim on the point of honour, that one exposes his life, and that all military men live in continual peril. He who has no quarrel may enter into one at any time with any of those people who only seek an opportunity to signalize their prowess, and to make themselves the subject of conversation. However moderate he may be, he cannot, without forfeiting this false honour, either avoid a quarrel by an explanation, or refuse to any one who may request it, and who wishes to fight. As yet no power has been found sufficient to root out a custom so barbarous. *Editor's note: Fenelon illustrates so poignantly, the necessity for parents and teachers to clearly define the true characteristics of virtue and honour and expose the immoral behaviors that culture and custom have paraded as acceptable. Virtue to Fenelon was understood in a classical sense, which included the eleven moral virtues of courage, temperance, liberality, magnificence, magnanimity, honour, gentleness, truthfulness, wittiness, friendliness and justice. (cf. Aristotle, "Nichomachean Ethics", 2.7.)*

See, then, how powerful are the prejudices of education; they will do much more for virtue when they shall be supported by reason, and by the hope of the kingdom of heaven. The Romans, of whom we have already spoken, and before them the Greeks, in the early time of their republic, brought up their children in contempt of selfish ambition and of idleness; they brought them up to esteem one glory, to desire not to possess riches, but to overcome the kings who possessed them, and to believe that they could only be happy by the practise of virtue. This spirit was so strongly established in those republics, that it enabled them to carry into execution, plans the most incredible, and to perform achievements the most stupendous, according to these maxims, so contrary to those of all other people. The examples of the martyrs, and of others amongst the first Christians, of all sex, condition, and of all ages, clearly evinces that the grace of God, joined to the force of education, was able to leave impressions still more forcible on the faithful, and to make them despise and contemn whatever belonged to the body.

Seek, then, the most agreeable manner, and the most striking comparisons, to convince children that our bodies are like the beasts, and that our souls are like the angels. Represent a rider mounted on a horse which he guides; say that the soul is, in respect to the body, what this rider is to his horse. Finish by saying that the soul is very weak and very miserable, when it suffers itself to be carried away by the body, as by a furious horse, which throws his rider into a precipice. Make them remark, that beauty of person is like a flower which opens itself in the morning, and at night fades, and is trodden under foot; but that the soul is the image of the immortal God. There is, you will add, an order of things much more excellent, than that which we see with our mortal eyes, for we see every thing here below subject to change and corruption. To make children feel that there are things real, which the eyes and the ears cannot perceive, we should ask them if they have ever seen the wisdom of that person? Then ask of what color is it? Does it make much noise? Have you touched it? Is it cold or hot? The child will laugh; he will do so when asked the same questions on the mind; he will appear quite astonished that we should ask him of what color is his mind; whether it be round or square. Thus, you may make him remark that he knows things which are very true, but which he can neither see, nor touch, nor hear, and that those things are spiritual. But we must enter very cautiously upon these discourses with young children. I propose them here only for those whose curiosity and reason lead you, in spite of yourself, to these questions. We must be guided according to the opening of their minds, and according to their wants.

With regard to young ladies, endeavour to limit their ardour for instruction within its due boundaries; and teach them, that a proper moderation in this respect is not less expected of them, and is not a less amiable trait in their character, than their extreme delicacy in avoiding every thing that could wound their unaffected innocence. *Editor's note: Young girls need to learn at an early age that one of their highest callings is that of being the completion to man, his partner in this life, to model and reflect the image of God. This thought is among the most ennobling qualities to be etched upon the minds of our young girls. This is not to suggest that women should not pursue the academic preparations necessary to reach a level of excellence in the field of study in which God has gifted them. It is also not to suggest that women who are single should feel inferior. On the contrary, whether married or single, a woman should fulfill her role of completion to man as God provides opportunity; first, in her family, and then if God so leads, in some capacity that supports and strengthens endeavours for the kingdom of God. Young girls need to learn from an early age that in the beautiful design of relationships, God has uniquely gifted them to fill a void in the life of man that could not otherwise be filled. It is in this fulfillment of roles, that the image of God is clearly seen in the grace and beauty of a woman, which becomes the standard for our young girls to follow. Today however, the boundaries of womanhood and manhood have been amalgamated to such an extent that a woman's pursuit of career goals is no longer based upon the standards of Scripture. I believe that Fenelon's reference to limiting a girl's ardour for instruction within its due boundaries, must be seen today in connection with the standards of modesty, subjection, a meek spirit, sobriety, and good works. i Tim. ii. 8-15.*

It is a wonderful knowledge a girl possesses, that her soul is the true image of Almighty God, and that the body has been gifted with the most wonderful qualities, all framed by an omnipotent and all-wise God. She is not to be blind that she was also born with inclinations that are constantly militating against reason; that she is deceived by pleasure, carried away by sallies of passion, and that her body, her inferior contrary to the dictates of reason, assumes the reins, and, like a high-mettled horse, runs away with its rider; whilst, on the contrary, it is the duty of the soul to maintain dominion, to dictate the law, and direct the operations of the body. She will perceive the origin and cause of this disorder in Adam's fall, and this history will make her look for the coming of a Saviour or Redeemer, to reconcile man with his offended and justly irritated Creator. This is the foundation and whole ground of her early instruction.

To enable young persons better to understand the mysteries, the actions, and maxims of Jesus Christ, it will be very useful to get them to read the holy gospels. You must, therefore, begin betimes to prepare them for the Word of God, by instilling a passion to search for the beautiful and redeeming truths it contains.

At the same time we should bring the imagination to aid the understanding, to give them a charming image of the truth of Christ, which would not be seen without this help. We should paint to them celestial glory, such as the apostle John represents it to us; all tears dried up; no more death; no more grief or crying; no sighs will escape us; all evil will be passed away; an eternal joy will flow over the hearts of the blessed, as the waters flow over the head of a man immersed in the depth of the sea. Show that glorious Jerusalem, of which God will himself be the sun, to light the days without end, in one uninterrupted flow of peace, in a torrent of delights, where we shall be refreshed by the waters of the fountain of life, where all will be gold, pearls, and precious stones. I well know that all these images attach to sensible things; but after having awakened the children by a spectacle so beautiful, in order to render them attentive, we must make sure of these means, which we have already touched, to lead them to things spiritual.

Give them to understand that we are here on this earth like travellers in an inn, or under a tent; that the body will perish, that we can slow its corruption only a few years, but that the soul will take its flight to that celestial country where it will live forever as God lives. If we could give children the habit of looking with pleasure upon these grand objects, and of judging of common things in comparison of these high hopes, we would find infinite difficulties removed from our hands.

I would also endeavour to give them strong impressions on the resurrection of the body. Recall to them the history of the resurrection of Lazarus, and afterwards that of Jesus Christ, and of his familiar appearances, during forty days, before so many persons. Finally, prove that it cannot be difficult to Him who has made man, to renew his existence. Do not forget the comparison of the grain of wheat which we sow in the earth and which becomes rotten, that it may in the end grow and multiply, and bear much fruit.

Teachers must not imagine that children will learn these lessons by heart. This would have no other purpose, than to turn Christianity into an affected language, at least into irksome and displeasing formalities. We ought only to aid their understanding, and to put them in a way of discovering these truths of themselves; for thus they will take greater satisfaction in their own discoveries, and will remember them with greater facility. We must avail ourselves of every opening, to render more clear and easy what as yet they only see and understand confusedly.

You must ever recollect that there can be nothing more dangerous than to speak to children concerning the contempt of the present life, without at the same time shewing them, by the uniformity of your conduct and conversation, that you are delivering the real sentiments of your heart. In every period of life, example has an astonishing influence, but in infancy it is everything. The great delight of children is to imitate others; as yet they have acquired no habit of their own, hence they can with the greater facility imitate those of others. Moreover, as they are incapable of judging of the merits of a thing by themselves, they chiefly form their judgments from what they observe in those who propose it to them, very little indeed from the reasons they themselves are able to produce. Actions have a far greater weight, and leave a far stronger impression than words; if therefore they see persons act differently to what they pretend to teach, they will learn to look upon Christianity as ceremonial, and upon virtue as impracticable. It is to this end that our children need to see the soul of Christianity, if I may be allowed to use this expression: to maintain a sovereign contempt for this life, and a great affection for the next.

CHAP. VIII.

Instruction On The Decalogue, And On Prayer.

The principle object, that we ought incessantly to keep before the eyes of children, is Jesus Christ, *the Author and Finisher of our faith*, *Heb xii. 2.* the centre of all, and our only hope. I do not mean here to say in what manner we ought to instruct them on the mystery of the incarnation. When the principles are formed, we must reform all the judgments and all the actions of the person whom we instruct, according to the model of Jesus Christ, who took a body like ours, to show us how to live, and how to die; showing us in his humanity what we ought to believe and practise. It is not necessary at every moment to compare the sentiments and actions of a child with the life of Jesus Christ. This comparison would become fatiguing, indiscreet, and troublesome; but we should accustom children to consider the life of Jesus Christ as our example, and his Word as our law. Choose among his discourses and actions, those most adapted to children. If they are impatient and intolerant at suffering any inconvenience, recall to their minds Jesus Christ on the cross. If they resolve not to undertake any disagreeable labour, show them Jesus Christ working as a carpenter to support his mother. If they be desirous of praise and esteem, speak to them of the shame and insults which were heaped upon our Saviour; for he took upon himself the form of a servant and humbled himself, and became obedient unto death, even the death of the cross. If they cannot agree with those around them, represent Christ conversing with sinners and the most abominable hypocrites. If they testify any resentment, hasten to represent to them Jesus Christ dying on the cross, crying, *father forgive them for they know not what they are doing;* even for those who put him to death. If they suffer themselves to be carried away by an immodest joy, paint to them the sweetness and the modesty of Christ, whose whole life was a reflection of the purest thoughts and motives. Teach them to think upon things that are pure, lovely, just, and holy; for as a man thinketh in his heart so is he. Finally, represent to them what Jesus Christ would think, and what he would say of our conversations, amusements, and the most serious occupations, if he were still visible amongst us.

What would be our astonishment, you may say to her, if, on a sudden, Jesus Christ should appear in the midst of us, whilst we are living in so profound forgetfulness of his law? But is this any thing more than what will befall every one of us at the hour of death, and the whole world when the time for the general judgment shall arrive? Then depict to her awakened imagination the general confusion and convulsion of the whole world:—the sun obscured—the stars falling from the firmament—the consuming elements running in liquid fire, and the foundations of the earth shaken to the very centre. With what eyes then, you will add, ought we to regard this heaven which covers us—this earth which bears us—these edifices which we inhabit—and all these other objects which surround us, since they are reserved only for fire? Let us fix not our hope on earthly things. Show them afterwards the tombs open, where the remains of the dead will be assembled; Jesus Christ descending on the clouds in great power and majesty; the book of consciences opened, in which will be written the most secret thoughts of our hearts; the sentence that will be pronounced before all nations and ages; the glory which will then open itself to crown eternally the just, and to make them reign with Jesus Christ upon the same throne. Finally, declare to them the lake of fire and brimstone, the night of darkness, and that eternal horror, that grinding of teeth, and that pain in common with the demons, which will be the everlasting portion of the wicked.

Do not fail to explain to your pupils at length the ten commandments. Teach them, that these two tables compose the abridgment of the law of God, and that in the gospel they can find more clearly and fully expressed what they can only deduce from the decalogue by remote inferences. Shew them that it is impossible to keep the law, but in fact it is the law that teaches us that we are guilty of sin; for without the law there would be no knowledge of sin. It is the Spirit that gives life and the grace of God that sustains us. It is not in escaping the corruption of this world, by quitting all, and retiring into solitude, that we escape the corruption of this world. Nay, on the contrary; victory over sin occurs when we put to death the deeds of the body through the help of the Spirit. *The letter killeth, but the spirit giveth life;* that is to say, the mere observance of outward forms is useless if not animated by the Spirit. Render this language clear and sensible—make them understand that God is to be honoured with the heart, and not with the lips only; that ceremonies may be regarded as the expression of the various acts of religion; that they nourish and excite devotion; but that ceremonies are not religion itself; religion must be in the soul; God seeks to be adored in spirit and in truth; we must love him interiorly, and we must behold in nature, only God and ourselves. He needs not our words or our postures, nor even our money; that which he desires is ourselves.

Let us finish by saying, that all those who cry Lord, Lord, will not enter into the kingdom of heaven; but, if we do not imbibe those true sentiments produced by the love of God in our souls, such as renouncing extravagance, selfishness, and the allurements of this world, we make but a phantom of Christianity to deceive ourselves and others.

God wills, we should say to the child, that we shall pray to him for grace, not because he is ignorant of our wants; but because he wishes to subject us to a demand, which excites us to acknowledge that want; it is thus an humiliation of our hearts, an acknowledgement of our misery and of our nothingness, it is that confidence in his goodness which he demands of us. This prayer, which he desires we should make, consists principally in the intention and desire; for he has no need of our words, for the spirit maketh intercession for us with groanings which cannot be uttered, though words mingled with humility are a mixture pure and sweet. We ought to be cautious, because praying with many words leads often to a recital that is aimed to please man rather than a plea for help from God. On the other hand, these words may nevertheless be very useful, for they excite in us thoughts and sentiments, if we are attentive to them. It is for this reason that Jesus Christ has given us a form of prayer. What a consolation to know from Jesus Christ himself, in what manner his Father wills that we should pray to him? Of what force must those demands be, which God himself puts into our mouth! Will he not grant that to us, which he himself teaches us how to ask? After this, show how simple and how sublime this prayer is; how short, and full of all that we can expect from above.

Concerning the Lord's Supper, parents ought to guard against casual partaking without the child evincing a true understanding of eternal life. It ought to be a long time expected, that is to say, we ought to make the child hope for it from his earliest infancy, as a most wonderful privilege. I believe that it would be well to render the effect as solemn as possible, that we should appear to have our eyes fixed on the child during those days—that we esteem him happy, that we take part in his joy, and that we expect from him a conduct above his age, for an action so great.

CHAP. IX.

REMARKS ON SEVERAL DEFECTS OF YOUNG CHILDREN.

We have still to specify several faults that are not uncommon in certain children, and to mark the care that should be taken to prevent them. In their tears, which they can at pleasure command, there is generally in the commencement a great deal of habit. Not to notice these assumed airs of affectation and sensibility, in which vanity and deceit have so great a share, is perhaps the most effectual method of reforming them.

We must also endeavour to regulate all attachments that are filled with over-charged and exaggerated compliments, and adulation; all this spoils their character, and makes them find every thing that is grave and serious both dry and austere. Care must even be taken to teach them to deliver their sentiments in a concise and accurate manner. True genius consists in retrenching from our conversation every thing trivial, and in saying a great deal in few words, whilst some say very little in a multiplicity of words. They erroneously take a facility of speaking, and a vivacity of imagination, for sterling wit; they make no selection of their thoughts, and reduce to no kind of order the subjects they wish to discuss; they are much too animated on every thing they wish to say; and where is the wonder, if their passion makes them speak too hastily and too verbosely. Pains must be taken to teach our young ladies to draw inferences, to examine and select their ideas, to express themselves with conciseness and precision, unless they have learned the grand secret of silence and reserve.

Not unfrequently a mother, who is prejudiced in favour of a particular director, will not rest content till her daughter places herself under the same guidance; and this she does through policy, though contrary to her own inclination. Above all things, a daughter should never be able to see in a parent, that she wishes to give her a turn for the religious state. This idea would remove all confidence due to parents, and would make the daughter believe that she was not beloved; it would agitate her mind, and compel her to act a forced and disguised character for many years. When young persons have had the misfortune of habitually disguising their sentiments, the true method of disabusing them, is to instruct them solidly in the maxims of true prudence; as the best mode of disgusting them of frivolous fictions of romances, is to instil into them a taste for useful and entertaining histories. Unless you can give them a reasonable curiosity, they will indulge, beyond all doubt, an improper curiosity. In the same manner, if you do not frame their minds to true prudence, they will attach themselves to that which is false, to finesse and cunning.

Shew them by examples how they may, without the least shadow of deceit, be discreet, provident and careful, how they may employ means in themselves honourable to secure success. Tell them, that prudence, in the first place, consists in speaking little, in shewing greater diffidence of ourselves than of others, but not in making false speeches, or acting double characters. Openness of heart, rectitude of conduct, and a general reputation for probity, will secure more confidence and esteem, and of course more, even temporal, advantages than any deep laid or crooked policy. How much does this judicious probity mark a person's merit and character; and what consideration can better fit them for the most important undertakings?

Do not forget to shew how very mean and despicable is this crafty and disguised spirit. We are only cunning when we wish to be concealed, when the object we envy is a trifle we feel ashamed of mentioning, or a passion which is in itself attended with dangers. When we wish for nothing more than what we ought and what we lawfully may desire, we candidly express our desires, and with moderation make use of open and approved means to accomplish our wishes. Is there any thing more sweet and convenient than sincerity; to be ever tranquil, to live in constant harmony with ourselves, to have nothing to fear, nothing to invent? Whilst, on the other hand, a person given to dissimulation, is in perpetual agitation of mind: she is exposed to remorse and danger, and under the deplorable necessity of covering one artifice, with a thousand others.

But besides a series of shameful troubles, that are their torments, these designing and cunning persons are not able so effectually to cloak themselves and their dispositions, as to escape detection. Sooner or later they are sure to pass for what they are. If in some insulated action the world can become a dupe to their artifice, it never can to the general body of their actions; there is always some unguarded spot in the veil under which they think to live concealed that betrays them, and leaves them open to just surmises and suspicions. Frequently themselves become the dupes of the very persons they wished to deceive; for, whilst they only pretend to admire others, they imagine themselves esteemed, although they are sovereignly despised. At best they cannot secure themselves against suspicions, and what is more contrary to personal enjoyment than to see ourselves every where suspected? Detail these instructions and reflections as occasions shall present themselves, and in proportion to the necessities and abilities of your pupils.

Observe, moreover, to them, that this finesse always originates in a mean heart and a base spirit. Persons are cunning purposely to conceal themselves. They are either not the characters they ought to be, and take unworthy means to obtain their ends, ignorant how to carry the point by more honourable means. Teach children the absurdity of certain mean tricks or fetches, which they see practised, and which are sure in the end to cover those that practise them with infamy, and do not fail to make them ashamed of themselves, as often as you surprise them in any act of dissimulation. Deprive them occasionally of what they are passionately fond of, if they attempt to acquire it by trick and artifice; and declare at the same time, that they shall have it when they ask openly and frankly for it. Bear patiently with their little weaknesses, that they may have courage to disclose them. Mauvaise honte, or unbecoming shame, is of all others the most dangerous, and ought to be remedied as soon as ever perceived; for this one fault, if in its earliest stages it be not attended to, will render every other evil incurable.

In this refinement of deceit, there is a greater degree of baseness in the character than in ordinary artifices and dissimulations. These refined deceivers pretend to justify to their own consciences their craft, whilst others, less dishonest, do not aim at deceiving themselves, but merely at deceiving their neighbour. Tell them that God is truth; that to sport with the majesty of God; that, to avoid this evil, we ought not to speak much, but to be very precise and exact in our expressions; that we should be careful never to say any thing that is not strictly correct, to shew our respect for truth.

On this account, never imitate those inconsiderate persons who can applaud and commend children, when they remark a great degree of wit and ingenuity in their little artifices. So far from admiring these designing tricks, and appearing pleased, reprimand them severely for the same; and endeavour to hinder the success of their cunning, that experience may give them a different bias. By praising children for faults of this description, you equivalently teach them a very erroneous principle, that cunning and deceit are marks of superior abilities.

CHAP. X.

The Vanity of Beauty And Of Dress.

Children are born with an intense desire of pleasing. Hence it is, particularly with girls, that they aspire so much after beauty, and all the exterior graces, and are so fond of dress. A head-dress or a ribbon, a curl a little higher or lower, or the choice of a color, are to them matters of high importance. *Editor's note: Though Fenelon's characterization may be true to some degree, I would not limit this flaw to girls, nor place every child into this category. It should be remembered that Fenelon lived during the 17th century.*
These things are carried much farther in our nation (France) than in any other; the changeable mood which reigns amongst us causes a continual variety of fashions; thus they add to the love of dress, that of novelty, which has strange charms for their minds. These two follies uniting together, destroy all distinctions in society, and wholly derange the

morals of the people. As soon as restrain is set aside in dress or furniture, affectation only remains.

This ambition is the ruin of families, which brings with it corruption of morals. On one side ambition excites in persons of low birth the passion of speedily acquiring a fortune, which they cannot do without sin, as the Holy Spirit assures us. On the other side, persons of quality finding themselves without resources, are guilty of horrible wickedness and meanness to support their expenses; by which they insensibly extinguish honour, faith, integrity, and good feeling, even among the nearest relatives and acquaintance.

Study then, to make children understand how the honour which is derived from good conduct, is more estimable than that which is drawn from the dressing of the head or from the figure. Beauty, you will say, deceives the person who possesses it more than those who are dazzled by it; it troubles and intoxicates the soul. They more weakly idolize themselves, than the most blind lovers are of the object of their passion.

Beauty can only be hurtful, if it be not upheld by merit and virtues. She can only hope to marry a young fool, with whom she will be unhappy, at least, if her wisdom and her modesty do not make her seek amongst men, a mind well regulated and sensible as to solid qualities. Those persons who draw all their glory from their beauty, soon become ridiculous; they arrive without perceiving it, at a certain age, when their beauty fades—and they are charmed with themselves, though the world, far from being so, is disgusted with them. In effect, it is as unreasonable to attach ourselves only to beauty, as it is to wish to rest all merit in our strength of body, as barbarians and savages do.

From beauty let us pass to dress. True graces do not depend on affected ornaments. It is true, that we should seek propriety, proportion, and decency in the dress necessary to cover our persons. But, after all, those garments which cover us, and which we may render convenient and agreeable, can never be ornaments which give true beauty.

I would even make young girls observe the noble simplicity which appears in statues, and in other ancient figures which remain to us of the Greek and Roman women; they would see there, how agreeable and majestic, the hair knotted up neatly from behind, and the long flowing draperies appear.

True grace follows nature, and never restrains it. But Fashion, that public tyrant, destroys—it aims always at being perfect, and never finds itself so. It would be reasonable if it only changed after having found a greater perfection, and a greater degree of taste in the commodity; but to change only for the sake of change, and without ceasing, is only to seek inconstancy and inconvenience, rather than true politeness and good taste. Generally speaking, fashions are governed wholly by caprice. Thus, minds, the most frivolous and least instructed, lead others. They neither choose nor abandon a thing by rule. It is sufficient for a thing to be a long while in fashion, to be so no longer; and that another, how ridiculous soever it may be, having a title to novelty, should take its place, and be admired. After having displayed this foundation, demonstrate the rules of christian modesty. Jesus Christ teaches us to place all our virtue in the fear and diffidence of ourselves. Have a horror, then, for an uncovered bosom, and for all other immodest actions, so extremely offensive to christian modesty. Though we should even commit these faults without any impure passion, the least we can say is, they proceed from vanity, and from an inordinate and unjustifiable desire of pleasing. We can neither justify our vanity before God, nor before man, for conduct so bold, so inconsiderate, so scandalous, and so contagious to others. Can this blind desire of pleasing at any rate become a christian soul, which should esteem as idolatry whatever tends to turn her away from the love of her Saviour? Is it not to excite the passions of men? It is an oral and a subtle poison. Girls need to know to what danger they expose themselves, and how they are despised by wise persons, when they thus forget that true beauty is that of a meek and quiet spirit

which is in the sight of God of great
price. Let her know how to possess a
quiet spirit, and how to conduct herself.
This quality which is so rare, will make
her happy in herself, beloved and
admired by others, and distinguish her
above her peers. Nothing is estimable
but good sense and solid virtue.

CHAP. XI.

INSTRUCTION TO WOMEN ON THEIR DUTIES.

It is now time to descend to the detail of those qualifications which a woman should most undoubtedly possess, and to enquire what will be her employments. She is charged with the education of her children: of sons, until they come to a certain age; of the daughters, until they marry or enter into the service of the Lord; of the conduct of the domestics, of their manners, of their service, of the detail of expense, of the means of doing every thing with honour and economy; sometimes to manage estates and receive rents.

The science of women, like that of men, ought to be limited to that instruction which relates to their duties. The difference of their employments ought to make that of their studies. A woman desirous of knowledge, will feel that this is giving very limited bounds to her curiosity; she deceives herself in this, and it is because she knows not the importance and the extent of those duties in which I propose to instruct her. What discernment, yea, what inestimable knowledge will be necessary to possess, in order to enter into the nature and the dispositions of each of her children; to find the most proper manner of conducting herself with them, in order to understand their mood, their inclination and their talents; to guard against their growing passions, to induce them to good habits, and to cure their errors? What prudence ought not she to have, to acquire and preserve an authority over them, without losing their friendship and confidence? And is it not also necessary that she should be fully acquainted with those persons whom she has about them? Undoubtedly the mother of a family ought to be fully instructed in the Scriptures; and she should have a mind matured, firm, regulated, and experienced in government.

I do not here explain all that women ought to know for the education of their children, because this memorial of it is sufficient to make them feel how extensive is the knowledge which they ought to have.

The ancient Greeks and Romans, who were so intelligent, generally speaking, and so polished, made the study of economy a considerable branch of their education. The first geniuses among them have written, from their own experience, treatises, which we read at present, on the different minute details of agriculture. We are not ignorant that their illustrious conquerors did not disdain a country life, and, returning from the honours of a triumph, they resumed the management of the plough. This conduct is so foreign to our modish refinement, that were there any room to doubt the credibility of these historians, many would disbelieve the fact, as overcharged and impossible. But is there any thing unnatural in the thought, that these illustrious victors, who were so active during war in defending or extending the limits of their country, should have thus exerted themselves with the design of cultivating it in the bosom of peace: for of what advantage is victory, unless to reap the fruits of peace?

It is undoubtedly necessary to possess a more powerful and cultivated understanding, in order to instruct ourselves thoroughly in all the arts which relate to economy, and to be in a state to govern a whole family, which is, as it were, a little republic, than to reason about fashions, and to exercise ourselves in the little arts of conversation. Accustom children from their infancy to keep something under their own management, to settle accounts, to see how every thing is bought, and how everything should be turned to profit: but take great care that this economy degenerate not into parsimony and avarice. Shew them how ridiculous and absurd all that are guilty of this base passion must appear. The gains of avarice are little, the disgrace it entails very great. A reasonable wife ought only to seek in her frugality and industry to avoid the imputation of shame and injustice that attach to a prodigal and ruinous conduct. Our true motive in retrenching superfluous expenses should be, to enable us to perform more liberally what good friendship, or charity may require. A small loss may eventually become a great gain.

Say as much on neatness as on economy; accustom girls to suffer nothing about them which is unclean or disorderly. Make them remark the least disorder in the house; make them even observe that nothing contributes more to economy and propriety, than to keep every thing in its place and not to suffer any thing to remain dirty. This rule appears trifling, nevertheless it would profit a great deal if it were well attended to. What you have need of, you lose no time in seeking; in this there is neither trouble, nor dispute, nor embarrassment—you put your hand upon it immediately; and when you have done with it, you replace it where you had found it. This good order makes one of the principle points in neatness. Nothing strikes the eye more than to see every thing in its proper place. On the other hand, the place we give to every thing is that which best suits it, not only

on account of its agreeableness to the
eye; but still more for its preservation. It
is less used, and is less subject to be
spoiled by accident; it is even properly
preserved. For example, a vase will not
be dusty, or in danger of being broken,
when it is put in its place immediately
after it is used. The same spirit of
exactness, which makes us arrange
every thing in its place, also makes us
neat. Add to these advantages, that of its
being a means of keeping servants in
better order. Moreover, it is a great
object to render their service prompt and
easy, and so take from yourself the
temptation of being impatient on account
of the delay which arises from things
being deranged and not to be found. But
at the same time, be careful to avoid all
excess of elegance and arrangement.

Arrangement, when it is moderate, is a
virtue; but when we devote our time too
much to it, then it becomes trifling and
shows a want of mind. Good taste rejects
excessive delicacy. It treats small things
as small, and is not wounded by them.
You will laugh, then, in the presence of
children, at those trifles of which some

women are so fond; and which insensibly cause them such extravagant expenses. Accustom them to simplicity and propriety, which are easy to practise. Show them the best manner of doing every thing. In this is God well pleased.

CHAP. XII.

CONTINUATION OF THE DUTIES OF WOMEN.

For the care of a woman's household, nothing is better than to accustom children to it at an early age. Give them something to manage, on condition that they render you an account of it. This confidence will please them exceedingly, for young persons receive incredible pleasures when we begin to confide in them, and to make them enter into some real business. We see a fine example of this in the reign of Queen Margaret. This princess recounts in her memoirs, that the most lively pleasure she experienced in her life, was to perceive that the queen, her mother, began to converse with her when she was yet young, as if she had been a grown person. She felt herself transported with joy, at being taken into the confidence of the queen, and of her brother, the duke of Anjou, regarding the secrets of the state. She had known until then, only the plays of children. Suffer children even to commit some faults in these affairs, and be willing to sacrifice something for her instruction; make her gently remark what she should have done or said, to avoid the inconveniences into which she had fallen; relate to her your past experience, and be not afraid to tell her of the faults, similar to her own, which you made in your youth. By this means you will inspire her with confidence, without which education must be a constrained formality.

CHAP. XIII.

ON GOVERNESSES.

It is not to be doubted, but that some will find it totally impracticable to go the whole length of our plan, or to embrace the whole extent of our ideas, which are thrown out on paper without the least obstacle or difficulty. But although the plan, in its different parts, may not appear feasible, still it is the best method to approach as near as possible to perfection. Moreover, we are far from expecting to meet with perfect dispositions in children, or to be greeted by most fortunate of circumstances, to enable us to realize our plan. On the contrary, my design has been to furnish remedies for such children as are born with unfavorable dispositions. I offer here, to parents and governesses, methods the most simple and easy to facilitate the task of rectifying, as much as may be, the defects that usually occur in ordinary plans of education. In vain, will they, who insist upon these defective plans, look in this little work for means to make a neglected or ill conducted education succeed. This is more than can be expected. What more ought to be looked for, are certain, clear, easy rules, which, if properly observed, will form a good education. I confess that less may be done, and that less is frequently done for children, than what I here propose; but it must in candour be allowed, that we every day see how much youth is prejudiced by this gross inattention and neglect.

The road I present, though it may appear long, is the shortest, since it leads directly to where we want to go; the other road, which is that of fear, and of a superficial cultivation of the mind, however short it appears, is too long; for by it we never arrive at the true end of education, which is to persuade the mind, and to inspire it with a sincere love of virtue.

The major part of children, who have been educated after this defective manner, have to renew their education when they thought it quite completed. Sometimes, after they have made their debut in the world, after they have passed whole years in committing blunders, and blunders frequently irreparable, experience and their own good sense must discover to them all those essential maxims, which their unnatural and superficial education was not able to inculcate. Nor should it be omitted, that the first attention which we require should be paid to children's education, and which unexperienced persons look upon not only as very difficult, but even as impracticable, restrain many more unpleasant circumstances, and removes many very great obstacles, which, after a less cultivated education, would become totally insurmountable.

In executing this project, the persons employed ought ever to carry in their mind the principle end proposed. We have not so much endeavoured to point out what would require great talents in the execution, as to propose the easy and obvious means of avoiding the gross and common defects we have had so frequent occasion to endure. Frequently we have urgently solicited teachers, not to force their pupils too much, but to watch them, to inspire them with confidence, to answer their little questions with the greatest good-will and precision; not to rebuff their natural dispositions, that they may be better known, and to set them right with great sweetness of temper, as often as they commit any blunder or fault.—It is, however, very unreasonable, to suppose that a good education can be conducted by a raw, inexperienced, and ill qualified governess. Where can we find governesses equal to the task of understanding this plan, will be asked? How then can we hope to meet with persons that will be able to follow it? But I could wish to be distinctly understood. Whenever a person aims at giving a perfect plan of education for youth, rules, that are in themselves imperfect, cannot be expected to give satisfaction. Since it is not unreasonable to expect that a good education should be conducted by a bad governess, then I propose that it is not demanding too much to desire that she should have at least good sense, a rational accommodating temper, and a true fear and love of God. A governess of this description will find nothing in this present essay either subtle or hard to understand; and should it even happen, that some parts may be rather above her capacity, she will form a good idea of the general plan, which, of itself, will suffice. Let her read the treatise several times over. Let a parent take the trouble of perusing it with her. Allow her to dwell on any points that she may not clearly comprehend, or that appear to be in the least objectionable; give her the liberty of stopping you, whenever she does not understand you, and when she is not persuaded of its truth. When you have satisfied her mind, then set her upon the practise, and, as often as you observe her deviating from the rules of conduct here laid down, and which she has engaged to follow in the education of your child, mention it to her in secret, and in the manner that would least wound her feelings.* This close attention will at first

---

* When a discreet and well-qualified governess has been found, great attention should be shewn her, and great deference paid to her judgment; for, if a governess be not respected by the family in which she lives, she

cost you a great deal of trouble, but if you are you are the father or mother of the child, it is no more than what your essential and indispensable duty requires. But this trouble will not be of any long duration. The governess, if she possess only an ordinary share of common sense and good will, must, in one month, learn more, by your advice and her own experience, than by the most profound and elaborate discourses; and in a short time she will of herself, without any assistance, walk in the direct path that is here chalked out for her. You will also find yourself free from

---

can never be respected by her pupil; and, if a fond mother will by her interference counteract her plans, and frustrate her attempts, she ought, in justice to her governess, to dismiss her, as no possible credit to herself, or advantage to her pupil, can be derived from so thwarted an education. –Parents will, perhaps, excuse themselves with saying, that their interference is only in trifles, and that no bad consequences can be the result: but trifling as it may appear to them, it may not prove so in its consequences. Moreover, nothing should be mentioned in public, or before the pupil, that can in the least reflect on the governess, or tend to diminish her authority; the largest rivers are trifling at their source, and the most destructive conflagrations have been occasioned by a single disregarded spark.

a great share of trouble and anxiety, by the reflection, that the chief discourses which the governess will have occasion to make to her pupil on the most momentous affairs, are already prepared for her in these strictures, and that she will have little more to do than to avail herself of them. She will find in this essay a collection of little conversations ready made to her hand, on the most difficult heads of instruction, which she will have to instil into her pupil. It is a practical, not a speculative essay, which I here present her, and it will prove of infinite utility to direct her every step in this momentous undertaking.

There most undoubtedly will occur a difficulty, and that is, in finding persons, even of ordinary abilities, equal to this charge. This is an essential point; for the most easy and simple things cannot be brought about of themselves, and they are sure to be ill executed when attempted by persons of harsh and improper tempers. Make a choice then of some young person in your own family, or upon your own estates, or among your friends, or in some regular community, a person that you may judge, upon proper enquiry, capable of being formed to this important office. Keep her some time near your own person, to try her before you entrust her with a concern of such amazing responsibility.

But although the difficulty of finding governesses be great, it must be owned that there is another greater, the irregularity of the parents. Every thing is useless, if they themselves will not concur in this work. The whole foundation is, that they give to their children right maxims and edifying examples. This is what we can only hope for in a small number of families. We see in the greater number of houses only confusion, and changes; servants of various dispositions, amongst whom reigns much contradiction of mind, and in disputes with their masters. What a frightful school for children! Often a mother, who passes her time in pleasure, in going to the theatre, and in improper conversations, complains, in a grave tone that she cannot find a governess capable of educating her daughters. But what can the best education do for girls when they see before their eyes such a mother? And again, we often see parents, who, lead their children to theatres, and other diversions, which cannot fail to disgust them with a life of seriousness and occupation, in which even these parents wish to engage them. They thus mix poison with salutary food. They speak of wisdom; but accustom the lively imaginations of their children to the violent emotions caused by the impassioned representation of theatre and affecting music, which is sure to incapacitate them for all serious application. They excite in their breasts a taste for indulging their passions, and thus make all innocent amusements appear dull and insipid. After this, they still expect their children's education to succeed; and they look upon it as too rigid and too severe, unless diversified with this charming mixture of good and evil. Is it not imputing a false honour to ourselves, to desire a good education for our children, without choosing to take the trouble of it; or to subject ourselves to the rules necessary for it?

It is the charge of parents to prepare their children to be careful not to leave a taste for any vanity of this world. Without exposing her to trials that are dangerous in themselves, discover to her the thorns concealed under the false pleasures which the world gives, and show her how many persons are there unhappy in the midst of pleasures. Let us conclude with the portrait which the wise man has given us of a virtuous woman, *Proverbs xxxi.* * *Who shall find a virtuous woman? The price of her is as of things brought afar off, and from the uttermost coasts. The heart of her husband trusteth in her, and he shall have no need of spoils. She will render him good and not evil, all the days of her life. She has sought wool and flax, and hath wrought by the counsel of her hands. She is like the merchant's ship,*

---

* This beautiful portrait of a wise woman is painted by the Queen mother of King *Lamuel.* This name signifies *God with him*, and it is supposed by interpreters to be one of the names given to Solomon. Such was the character which the mother of Solomon wished to recommend as a suitable Queen for her royal son; a character that is beautifully drawn out in detail by Mons, Formey, in his *Philosophe Chretien*, vol. i. p. 295.

she bringeth her bread from afar. And she hath risen in the night, and given a prey to her household and victuals to her maidens. She hath considered a field, and bought it: with the fruit of her hands she hath planted a vineyard. She hath girded her loins with strength, and hath strengthened her arm. She hath tasted and seen that her traffic is good: her lamp shall not be put out in the night. She hath put her hand to strong things, and her fingers have taken hold of the spindle. She hath opened her hand to the needy, and stretched out her hands to the poor. She shall not fear for her house in the cold of snow: for all her domestics are clothed with double garments. She hath made for herself clothing of tapestry; fine linen and purple is her covering. Her husband is honourable in the gates, where he sitteth among the senators of the land. She made fine linen and sold it, and delivered a girdle to the merchant. Strength and beauty are her clothing, and she shall laugh in the latter day. She hath opened her mouth to wisdom, and the law of clemency is upon her tongue. She hath looked well to the paths of her house, and hath not eaten the bread of indolence. Her children rose up and called her blessed: her husband, and he praised her. Many daughters have accumulated riches: thou hast surpassed them all. Favour is deceitful and beauty is vain: the woman that feareth the Lord, she shall be praised. Give her the fruits of her hands; and let her works praise her in the gates.

Although, from the extreme difference of manners, from the conciseness and boldness of the figures, the language must, at first sight, appear obscure; still, if we examine it with a little more attention, we shall discover in it a style so lively and full, that it will be impossible not to feel charmed with the beauty and natural simplicity. But what I wish most should be admired, is the authority of Solomon, the wisest of men, or rather the authority of the Holy Ghost himself, who speaks by the mouth of the wise man, and extols in terms so very magnificent this simplicity of manners, this economy and industry in women of distinction, which we also have in the present strictures on education endeavoured in the most forcible terms to press upon our readers.

EPISTLE FROM MADAME DE MAINTENON.

This correspondence, and this pious dialogue between Madame de Maintenon and Fenelon, gained more and more for the future author of *Telemachus* the regard and esteem of one who reigned with uncontrolled power: she frequently reverted with pleasure, in her advanced years, to the sentiments she had then experienced.

"I have often since wondered," writes she, "why I did not select the Abbe de Fenelon as the guide of my conscience, when his manners charmed me so much, and when his mind and virtues had so influenced me in his favor." She, more than any other woman in her position, required the society of a man in all points equally attractive and superior, surrounded as she was by common-place spirits, and by empty coldness. "Ah!" (she wrote at one period to her favorite niece), "alas that I cannot give you my experience, that I could only show you the weariness of soul by which the great are devoured; the difficulty which they find in getting through their days. Do you not see how they die of sadness in the midst of that fortune which has been a burden to them? I have been young and beautiful; I have tasted many pleasures; I have been universally beloved. At a more advanced age I have passed years in the association of talent and wit, and I solemnly protest to you, that all conditions leave a frightful void."

This friendship of Madame de Maintenon for the most fascinating man in the kingdom, inspired the monarch with the idea of recompensing Fenelon for his success in the education of his grandson, by the gift of the Abbacy of Saint-Valery. The king in person announced to him his gracious intention, and made many excuses for bestowing upon his services so tardy and disproportionate a reward. All things seemed to smile upon Fenelon. The heart of Madame de Maintenon seemed to have gained for him the love of the entire Court.

FENELON'S EPISTLE TO A LADY OF DISTINCTION, ON THE EDUCATION OF HER DAUGHTER.

Madam,

As you are so very urging in your request, I will endeavour to give you my ideas on paper, relative to the education of your daughter.

Had you many to educate, the task would be embarrassing, as your connexions in life oblige you to absent yourself more from your family than you would wish. In that case, you should choose some school where the education of boarders is studiously attended to. But as you have an only daughter to educate, and as God has rendered you perfectly adequate to the undertaking, I think she may receive from you a better education than in any school. The eyes of a wise, tender and christian mother, undoubtedly discover blemishes that would escape others. Frequently, mothers have not learning requisite to educate their daughters, or if they have, they do not strengthen it by the example of a serious and christian conduct; for all that a mother can say to a daughter, is speedily done away by what the daughter observes in her mother's actions. With you, Madam, the reverse is precisely the case. Your first thought is to love and serve God; Christianity, with you, not only claims but possesses the first place in your heart, and you will only have to instil into your daughter what she will see you constantly practise yourself. Hence I must except you from the general rule, and prefer you, for her education. Great are the advantages that your daughter will receive from being educated under your eye. The most subtle of poisons is vanity; and even in christian circles, if the greatest precaution be not taken, this vice, so dangerous for young persons, may have its charms. She would hear the scholars speaking of the world as of a scene of enchantment; and nothing can leave a more injurious impression on the mind than this deceitful image. It is held up at a distance, as the centre of pleasure and felicity; whilst its disappointments, bitters, and disgusts, are carefully concealed. The world never dazzles so much as when viewed at a distance, before it has been really seen, and without being forewarned of its seduction. Hence, I would fear worldly Christians more than the world itself. A girl who has been disengaged from the world by being ignorant of it, and in whose heart virtue has not had time to strike deep roots, will soon be tempted to believe that the charms of a worldly life have been studiously concealed from her. She leaves home like a person who has been brought forth from a dark dungeon where he has been pent up all his life, and exposed to open day. Nothing can be more dazzling than this sudden transit from one extreme to another. Far better is it for a girl to be introduced by degrees to the manners of the world, under the protection of a discreet and virtuous mother who will only suffer her to see what is proper for her—who will point out as occasion shall offer the dangers of the world, and who will teach her by her own example, to use it with moderation, and as necessity requires. I esteem the

education given in good schools, but I
have decided preference to that given by
a learned and virtuous mother, if she
have it in her power to give the
necessary attendance. I conclude,
therefore, that your daughter is better
situated near you, than she can possibly
be in the very best school. But there are
very few mothers to whom I would
venture to give the same advice.

I allow that this education would be
attended with many dangers, unless you
take care in the choice of persons you
suffer to be about your daughter. Your
domestic occupations, and the duties of
civility abroad, will not permit you to
have your child always under your eyes.
You cannot always take her with you;
but I recommend you, to quit her as little
as possible. If you entrust her to light,
indiscreet, or disorderly women, they
will teach her more evil in eight days,
than you will be able to teach her good in
several years. These persons, who, for
the most part, have only received a very
moderate education themselves, will
educate your child in the same defective
manner. They will speak in her presence

with too great freedom, and your daughter will not fail to notice every thing that is said or done, and will endeavour to do the same. They will lay down the most false and dangerous maxims. The child will hear slander, lying, suspicious and wrangling words; she will see jealousies, animosities, incompatibility of temper, and sometimes false and dangerous devotions without any correction of the grossest faults. These persons, moreover, are of a mean and servile spirit; they will not fail to please the child by base and dangerous flattery, and do every thing they can to insinuate themselves into the her good graces. I confess, that the education given by the most indifferent schools, would be superior to this domestic education; but I am supposing that you will never lose sight of your daughter, except in cases of absolute necessity, and that you will have a person on whom you can depend to take the responsibility in your absence. This person must have sufficient sense and virtue to know how to maintain a certain degree of authority sufficient to keep others that may be employed in their strict duty; to correct the child when necessary, without incurring her displeasure, and to acquaint you, at your return, of whatever is deserving your notice. I allow, that such a person is not easy to be found; but you must attend to this point, and do not refuse the necessary expense to make her situation as agreeable as possible. I know that you may, on many occasions, be disappointed; but you must rest satisfied with the essential qualifications, and tolerate such defects as may be mixed with these accomplishments. Without the assistance of a person of this description, believe me, you will never succeed in the education of your daughter.

As your daughter shows great quickness of parts, great facility, penetration, openness, and candour, I fear she may acquire a taste for ambition, and an excess of vain and dangerous curiosity. You will permit me, Madam, to make one reflection, which ought not to wound your extreme delicacy of feeling, as it does not regard you. Women in general are more passionately fond of the ornaments of the mind, than those of the body; and all those who are capable of scholarship, who have hopes of distinguishing themselves, betray a greater degree of eagerness for their books, than they possibly can for their dress. A lady who prides herself on her extensive knowledge and great superiority over the rest of her sex, finds her glory in despising the amusements and vanities that have such attractions for others. She thinks herself equal to form a solid judgment in even the most difficult occurrence. She flatters herself with knowing every thing, and of course is ever ready to decide. In every discussion, how much soever above her capacity, even in affairs of religion, she warmly and decidedly embraces one party and reprobates the opposite sentiment. Hence it happened, that all modern sects in their infancy made such astonishing progress by means of women, who have passionately supported and craftily insinuated their new-fangled doctrines. *Editor's note: Though the same can be said of men, this state of outspoken haughtiness in women is even more repugnant because it violates the charm, beauty, and grace that sets the woman apart from the man.*

It will therefore be necessary, incessantly to recall your daughter to a judicious simplicity. It will be enough for her to possess that knowledge of her faith and punctually to follow it in practise. She must only hear the Word of God and follow faithfully those who preach its truth. She must shun the conversation of indiscreet women who take upon themselves to argue points of doctrine; and she should be taught how unbecoming and dangerous this liberty is. She should hold in utter abhorrence all pernicious publications, without wishing even to examine why they are condemned. She should learn to be diffident of herself*, and to fear the snare of curiosity and presumption. She should

---

* Have you seen a man wise in his own conceit? There shall be more hope of a fool than of him.

Prov.xxvi. 12.

be earnest in her supplications to God, that she may become poor of spirit, frequently recollected, and at all times submissive. She should take pleasure in being corrected by her wise and discreet friends, even in her most decided judgments, and should learn the talent of listening with deference to others. I would far sooner have her learned in the manner of keeping the accounts of the house, than in the school disputes of theology. The virtuous woman, says the wise man, spins, and finds happiness in her own family.

I am perfectly confident, Madam, that you will be able, as occasions shall present themselves, to introduce well-timed reflections on the impropriety and indecency observable in others. These observations you must make, purposely to preserve your daughter from foundering against the same dangerous rock. But as authority of a mother must be carefully preserved, and as the wisest lessons do not always carry conviction to a daughter, when contrary to her own inclinations, it would be adviseable to engage ladies of approved merit in the world, and your true friends, to speak with you in the presence of your daughter on this subject, without appearing to allude to her in the most distant manner. These indirect instructions will, in all appearance, leave a more lasting impression on her mind, than all the discourses you could direct to her personally.

With regard to dress, I could wish you might be able to instil into your daughter's mind a true taste for moderation. It is, most enviable, and at the same time the most rare, to aim at that wise and just mediocrity, which will equally avoid both extremes; which will give to the world what the world can reasonably expect, without trespassing the limits which moderation has prescribed. True wisdom, with regard to furniture, equipage, and dress, is to avoid singularity, by avoiding all extremes. Dress yourself, you may say to your daughter, so as not to pass in the eyes of the world, as a slovenly person, without taste; but at the same time, let no affectation of dress, no pomp appear in your exterior: thus you will shew that you are possessed with reason and virtue superior far to your furniture, equipage, or dress; you will make use of them as the blessings of an ever kind Providence, without becoming their slave. She ought also to be made sensible, that however great riches a young lady may bring into a family, she must soon prove its ruin, if she introduce into it a passion for luxury, which no riches can satisfy. Endeavour at the same time to teach her to reflect on the distresses and miseries of the poor, to commiserate their situation, and to consider what a disgrace it is to humanity, that certain persons who live in the greatest opulence should put no limits to their extravagance, whilst they cruelly and unfeelingly refuse what is essentially necessary to the maintenance of the indigent. If you keep your daughter in a state below those of her own rank and age in life, you run the risk of alienating her affections from you. She may, perhaps in that case, feel a desire for what she sees and admires in others, and what she cannot acquire. She would be tempted to think that you were too parsimonious and too severe. She would, then, perhaps, be impatient to see herself at her own disposal, that she might have her fling in the vanity of the world. You would succeed far better in keeping her in the just medium, and this line of conduct must meet with the approbation of all prudent and sensible persons. She will then see that you wish her to have every thing that becomes her; that you deny her nothing through sordid economy, or a penurious spirit; that you have every proper consideration for her; and that your only wish is to preserve her from imitating the extravagance of certain persons, whose vanity know no bounds.

A young lady, who forms a connexion with a vain, irregular, and light character, may be said to make a sacrifice of all future happiness and contentment. To find a steady, wise, and discreet companion for life, she must be extremely proper and modest, and suffer nothing light or foolish to transpire in her conduct. For where is the man, who has any pretensions to wisdom and prudence himself, that can admire a young woman who, to judge from appearances, is full of vanity and conceit, and whose virtue is at best equivocal.

But your grand resource to implant in the mind true christian virtue, is to gain the heart of your daughter. Do not disgust her with piety by an useless severity: give her a proper degree of liberty, and suffer her to enjoy innocent amusements. Select for your daughter discreet and good companions, that will not corrupt her: let her have fixed hours of recreation, which will give no disrelish for serious pursuits the remainder of the day. Endeavour to excite in her breast an affectionate love for God, and teach her not to look upon him as merely an almighty and inexorable judge, whose eye is ever upon us, to watch, censure, and restrain us upon every occasion. Shew her how sweet is the service of the Lord, how he proportions his gifts and graces to our necessities, and how much he commiserated our weakness. Accustom her to address him as a tender and affectionate parent. Let her never look upon prayer as a troublesome and idle inactivity, where the mind is under a constant restraint, while the distracted imagination is ever wandering. Teach her that she ought frequently to turn her thoughts inwardly, to find her God, because his kingdom is within those who believe. At every hour, either of the day or night, we may speak with all simplicity to our good God, confess our faults, represent our necessities, and talk with him about the necessary measures for the speedy amendment of our faults. We ought to listen to God in the interior silence of the soul, saying: I will listen to the Lord within myself. We must endeavour to acquire the happy and excellent habit of walking always in his presence, and of doing all things, great or small, with cheerfulness, and for his sake; and as often as we perceive that we have lost sight of his presence, so often must we renew it. We must be patient with ourselves, and not feel disheartened at our light-mindedness and unfaithfulness; but be willing to confess our faults one to another, walking in light as he is in the light. It is then, and only then that we can have true fellowship with one another, as the blood of Jesus Christ cleanses us from all sin. Persons who limit themselves to a certain form of prayer, are before God, as they are before persons they respect, and whom they only see occasionally through formality, without either loving them, or being loved by them; the whole visit passes in ceremonies and compliments; both parties are uneasy, tired, and impatient to be set at liberty. Whereas persons truly interior are, with God, as with the most intimate friends: they do not measure their words, because they know to whom they are speaking: every thing proceeds from the simplicity and abundance of the heart. We speak to him of the most interesting subjects of his own glory and our salvation. We mention to him the faults we wish to fulfil, the temptations we wish to overcome, and the artifices of our own self-love we wish to repress. In a word, we tell him everything. This is no longer a ceremonial communion, but a free conversation of true friendship. Then God becomes a real friend; a parent, in whose breast a child finds consolation; a spouse, with whom, through grace, one and the same spirit is found to empower and fortify them. There we humble, without discouraging ourselves: we unite a sincere confidence in God, with a total diffidence of ourselves; there we never forget the correction of our faults, but we forget to listen to the deceitful counsels of self-love. If Madam, you instil and nourish this simple and solid piety into your daughter, she cannot fail of making most rapid progress. With respect,

I remain, & c.

Francois de Salignac de La Mothe Fenelon

ADDENDUM.

TELEMACHUS AND THE VIRTUOUS WOMAN.

The portrait of a discreet, virtuous, and accomplished woman, delineated by the inimitable limner, Fenelon, in the 22nd book of Telemachus, in the character of Antiope, and formed upon the system of education laid down in the present essay, must prove very acceptable.

A woman loveliest of the lovely kind,
In body perfect, and complete in mind.

"What chiefly pleases in Antiope, the object of your attachment," said Mentor to Telemachus, "is that suavity of disposition, which enhances her amiable simplicity and wisdom. She is not above working with her hands; she has a wise forethought, and provides against every contingency. She knows when it is proper to be silent: she is incessantly occupied, but never in a hurry, because each duty is performed in due time and order. The regularity of her royal father's household is her glory, which sets her off to far greater advantage than the uncommon charms of her person[*]. Although the superintendence of every concern to be entrusted to her, although it be hers to correct, to refuse, and to economize, (three things which generally draw down a great share of ill-will on most women) she has secured the affections of each individual in the family, because they could observe in her deportment neither caprice not positiveness, neither levity nor extravagance, as in other women. With a single glance of the eye she makes herself understood, and all are anxious to give her satisfaction. She is precise in her orders, and never commands any

---

[*] The whole of this beautiful portrait agrees perfectly well with Maria Theresa of Austraulia, Insanta of Spain, destined for the comfort of Lewis XIV. The Marechal de Gramont, on his return from his embassy to solicit the alliance in the name of the king, among other qualifications added, "qu'à peine l'avoit il entendu parler." The future conduct of this excellent and virtuous queen justified the flattering character that fame had sent before her to the French court.

thing that cannot be executed. When necessitated to find fault, she reproves with kindness, and at the same time encourages. The heart of her father, Idomeneus, rests sweetly upon her, as the fatigued traveller, exhausted with the scorching beams of the sun, finds the most sweet repose in the shade on the tender grass. I admire your choice, Telemachus; Antiope is a treasure worthy of being sought even in the remotest corners of the globe. Her person she never decks out with vain and extravagant ornaments, nor her mind with useless knowledge. Her imagination, though lively, is kept under proper restraint by her judgment. She never speaks but when necessity requires; and as often as she opens her mouth, persuasion and native graces drop from her lips. When she begins to speak, all are instantly silent. Their attention raises a modest blush on her cheeks, and makes her almost wish to supress what otherwise she could wish to advance. In a word, she is so silent, and so discreet, that we have very seldom heard her speak.

APPENDIX,

CONTAINING

INSTRUCTIONS FOR A MOTHER OR GOVERNESS.

FORMED AFTER

FENELON'S PLAN OF EDUCATION.

1. Study well the constitution and genius of your children.
2. Follow nature, and proceed easily and patiently.
3. Suffer not servants to be with them, much less to terrify them with frightful stories.
4. Give them a pleasing idea of good, and a frightful idea of evil.
5. Let their diet be plain and good, and their exercise and meals justly regulated.

6. Watch the first appearances of reason, and carefully cultivate them.

7. Labour sweetly to correct their childish passions and prejudices.

8. Use no dissembling arts to pacify or persuade them.

9. Recommend an open, sincere character, and shew a just abhorrence to duplicity.

10. If they be witty, do not flatter them; if dull, do not discourage them.

11. Endeavour to rectify their judgment, fortify their reason, and restrain their imagination.

12. To all their questions, give short and opposite answers.

13. Promote useful curiosity, but supress every sentiment of vanity and self-conceit.

14. Instil just principles of politeness, modesty, and every christian vanity.

15. Shew the deformity and baseness of a lie, and how detestable is the character of a liar.

16. Check their too impetuous desires, and habituate them to frequent privations.

17. Teach them to do all things in order, and with method, but nothing in a hurry.

18. Insinuate the principle of economy, but a hatred for parsimony.

19. Improve the feelings of their heart, by conducting them to objects in distress.

20. Let them see that personal charms are not to be compared with mental accomplishments.

21. Their dress and studies should both be regulated according to their rank in life.

22. Civility is due to all, familiarity to very few.

23. The less they make of themselves, the more they will be admired by others.

24. Teach them to copy, in themselves, what they most admire in their companions, and carefully to avoid what is particularly offensive.

25. A habit of industry and occupation will secure them from many temptations.
26. Make them virtuous in youth, and they will be a support to their parents in their old age.
27. Let virtue and religion have the first place in their hearts.
28. And their early years be sacred to piety.
29. Instruct them of how much greater value is their immortal soul than this perishable world.
30. And that sooner than risk the former, they must sacrifice the latter.

FINIS.

Recommended Reading From The Lamplighter Rare Collector's Series

The Basket of Flowers. Christoph Von Schmid
First written in the late seventeen hundreds, this book is the first in the **Lamplighter Rare Collector's Series** which gave birth to Lamplighter Publishing. Come to the garden with the godly gardener, James, and his lovely daughter, Mary, and you will see why Elisabeth Elliot and Dr. Tedd Tripp so highly recommend this rare treasure.

Stepping Heavenward. Elizabeth Prentiss
Recommended by Elisabeth Elliot, Kay Arthur, and Joni Eareckson Tada, this book is for women who are seeking an intimate walk with Christ. Written in 1850, this book will reach deeply into your heart and soul with fresh spiritual insights and honest answers to questions that most women and even men would love to have settled.

Titus: A Comrade Of The Cross. F. M. Kingsley
In 1894 the publisher of this book gave a $1,000 reward to any person who could write a manuscript that would set a child's heart on fire for Jesus Christ. In six weeks, the demand was so great for this book that they printed 200,000 additional copies! You and your family will fall in love with the Savior as you read this masterpiece.

Jessica's First Prayer. H. Stretton
What does a coffee maker have in common with a barefoot little girl? You will want to read this classic over and over again to your children as they gain new insights into compassion and mercy as never before.

A Peep Behind The Scenes. O. F. Walton
Behind most lives, there are masks that hide our hurts and fears. As you read, or more likely cry, through this delicate work, you will understand why there is so much joy in the presence of angels when one repents. Once you read it, you will know why two-and-a-half-million copies were printed in the 1800s.

Joel: A Boy of Galilee. ANNIE FELLOWS JOHNSTON

If you read *Titus: A Comrade of the Cross* and loved it, let me introduce you to *Joel*. This is a story about a handicapped boy who has to make a decision whether to follow the healer of Nazareth or the traditions of the day. This is a treasure you will talk about for years.

The Lamplighter. MARIA S. CUMMINS

Written in the 1800's when lamplighters lit the street lights of the village, this story will take you on a spiritual journey depicting godly character that will inspire and attract you to live your Christian life with a higher level of integrity and excellence. Mystery, suspense, and plenty of appealing examples of integrity and honor will grip the heart of anyone who reads this masterpiece.

The Inheritance. CHRISTOPH VON SCHMID

This is another classic by the author of *The Basket of Flowers*. Seeking first the Kingdom of God and His righteousness will be a theme that parents and children will see through the eyes of a faithful grandson and his blind grandfather.

The Hedge of Thorns. ANONYMOUS

Based on a true story about a little boy who will do almost anything to find out what is on the other side of a hedge of thorns. Enticed and frustrated, a child is about to learn why boundaries are a necessary part of God's plan for his life.

The White Dove. CHRISTOPH VON SCHMID

This is another classic by the author of *The Basket of Flowers* that will once again lay a beautiful pattern of godliness for all to follow. Surrounded by knights and nobles, thieves and robbers, this story will take parent and child to the precipice of honor, nobility, sacrifice, and the meaning of true friendship. If you enjoyed *The Basket of Flowers*, you will not want to miss *The White Dove*.

Melody, The Story of A Child. LAURA E. RICHARDS

An inspiring and beautifully written story that invites the reader to see life through the eyes of a most unusual child. Each chapter is filled with charming freshness as a blind child weaves her gift of "seeing" into the hearts of friend and foe alike. Themes: uncompromising love, discernment, childlike honesty, faith and forgiveness.

The Lost Ruby. CHRISTOPH VON SCHMID

Another classic that will teach children the important lesson of honesty regardless of the cost. Also included is one of Von Schmid's finest short stories, *The Lost Child*. This is a story that is filled with mystery and intrigue as the reader learns that God allows hardships for our good.

The Little Lamb. CHRISTOPH VON SCHMID

This story will teach our readers that all things do work together for good to them who love God. Parents and children will be filled with captivating suspense as they taste and see that the Lord is the God of the impossible.

Famous Boys and How They Became Great Men.

Today there is a cry among our leaders for children to be obedient, faithful, and true. This book will offer boys and young men hope for even the most despairing circumstances. Read how some of the greatest men in history turned hardships and heartaches into the seed beds of greatness.

The Beggar's Blessing. MARK HAMBY

A true story from the 1800s about a little girl who sacrificed her savings for a starving beggar. Full-color illustrations will capture the hearts of children as they learn that sacrifice is the cornerstone for surprising blessings. This is a story that you will never forget and is sure to become a children's classic!

The True Princess. ANGELA HUNT

This book is a classic that will teach children what makes a true princess in Jesus' eyes! Truly a treasure to be passed on to the next generation. Based on the Scriptural teachings of servanthood.

Life-Transforming Seminars. Audio, M. HAMBY

- The Strong-Willed Parent.
- The Angry Parent, Child, and Teen.
- Resolved Conflicts and Restored Relationships.
- Life Transforming Literature.

The Lamplighter Newsletter

Free and available upon request. Rich with biblical insights on marriage, parenting, book reviews, teaching ideas, mentoring boys and nurturing girls, and a special section devoted to "Let God's Creatures Be the Teachers."

Lamplighter Publishing.

P.O. Box 777
Waverly, PA 18471
1-888-A-Gospel

E-mail: lamplighter@agospel.com
Web site: www.agospel.com

Making ready a people prepared for the Lord.
Luke 1:17